OVERFLOWING INSPIRATION

SONGS AND POEMS OF PRAISE

MARYANN TOLSON

Published by Happy Jack Publishing, LLC

Copyright © 2016
by Maryann Tolson

All rights reserved. No part of this book may be used or reproduced in any manner without written permission except in the case of brief quotations embodied in articles and reviews. Unauthorized reproduction of any part of this work is illegal and punishable by law.

*The author attests that all photos used in this publication are royalty free or property of the author.

Copyright © 2016 Maryann Tolson
All rights reserved.
ISBN: 1-944104-09-7
ISBN-13: 978-1-944104-09-2

DEDICATIONS AND ACKNOWLDGMENTS

To my Father God who created me.

To my Savior Jesus Christ who died on the cross for me.

To the Holy Spirit who leads me and guides me into truth.

To Julie who spoke into my life through the Holy Spirit of God. She told me I was going to write many songs to encourage people everywhere.

To Momma Tayla who encouraged me to use my gift as a psalmist in her ministry. She also told me that there were many books in me.

To my pastors, Randy and Betty Waterman, who have been teaching me, loving me, and encouraging me to learn and grow for over 30 years. They encourage me to keep writing my books.

To my friend, Carol, who played the piano to a song I wrote and sang it with me.

To my husband who bought me a new printer and computer so I could go forward in my dreams.

To my boss, Cheryl Cross, who is my featured guest.

To House of Mercy who allows me to inspire staff as well as residents.

And to all those who allowed me to sing to them over the years.

Thank you to Beth Burgmeyer, my editor and publisher with Happy Jack Publishing.

CONTENTS

Part One: 1
   First Inspirational Songs

Part Two: 13
   Prayer Songs

Part Three: 16
   Trinity Songs

Part Four: 33
   Songs of Declaration & Anticipation

Part Five: 38
   Memory Poems of My Mom

Part Six: 51
   Poems for My Dad

Part Seven: 54
   My Boss, Cheryl Cross

Part Eight: 57
   Work Community

Part Nine: 214
   Family and Community

ABOUT MY SONGS

Some songs are short and some are longer. As you go through the journey with me you will see how my gift is developing and how it has developed through the years. With God's help it is getting better and better. This has been, and is, one exciting journey, and I'm sure there is better yet to come because God is so awesome

ABOUT MY CREATIVITY

First of all, being a poet is a gift from God. My creativity comes in many different ways: through smell, seeing different colors, seeing beautiful things, people, and hearing amazing stories. But for the most part, God's kindness flows through me and sometimes I just wake up inspired as God speaks to me in my dreams. God is so amazing, so amazing yes indeed

ABOUT PSALM 32:7

When I first read Psalm 32:7 I thought, what does the Bible mean when it says *thou art my hiding place thou shalt compass me about with songs of deliverance*. When I looked up compass in the dictionary, one of the definitions is a sense of direction. As I look over my life for the past 14 years, I can see how He compasses. As some of you read this book you may ask, "How can you say these are songs when they are so short?" To that I would say, "These songs are the beginning of learning how to use the gift that is inside of me."

.

PART ONE: FIRST INSPIRATIONAL SONGS

EVERYTHING THAT YOU HAVE BEEN THROUGH

Everything that you have been through
I will truly use you to tell others how I brought you through
Just reach deep inside and my spirit will lead and guide you
And show you how to help others too

I WAIT PATIENTLY FOR YOU

I wait patiently for you
I wait patiently for you
I wait patiently for you with a heart renewed
I seek your holy face
I feel your warm embrace
I lay here on my face and wait patiently for you
For you alone are true
For you alone are true
For you alone are true
I wait patiently for you

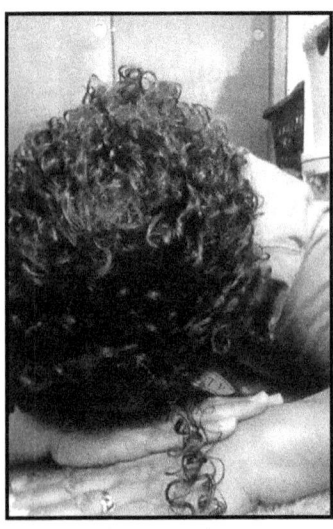

LET HEAVEN REJOICE

Let heaven rejoice and praise and sing
And glorify our great King
You died on the cross
To save the lost
Let us rejoice
You made the right choice

DON'T BE DOUBLE MINDED

Don't be double minded and unstable
You must believe that I am able
To see you through
When you don't know what to do
For I am your Father and you are my daughter

I HAVE FORGIVEN YOU

I have forgiven you
You must forgive yourself
I died on Calvary
To set my people free
Though your earthly father's not around
I, your Heavenly Father, can always be found

I PRAISE YOU

I praise you
You are the Holy one
I praise you for giving us your son
I praise you, you are worthy to be praised

LIFE AND DEATH

Life and death are in the power of the tongue
If you speak words of life
It will keep you out of strife

___YOU MUST PRAISE ME OR THE ROCKS WILL CRY OUT___

You must praise me or the rocks will cry out
You must praise me without a shadow of a doubt
When you feel like you want to pout
Just praise me with a shout
You must praise me or the rocks will cry out

When you feel like you want to quit
Just come before me and sit
You must praise me or the rocks will cry out
When the devil tells you a lie
And you feel like you're going to die
You must praise me or the rocks will cry out

___WHEN YOU'RE IN PAIN DON'T GO INSANE___

When you're in pain don't go insane
Just trust in me I'll set you free
When you're in doubt don't start to pout
Just rise and sing and praise your King

YOU CAN'T HIDE FROM ME

You can't hide from me because through you I can see
My word is like a light that shines in the darkest night
Just read my word and see, it will show you reality
That there is nothing, nothing, hid from me
Hid from me, there's nothing hid from me

WHEN I PRAISE YOU IT MAKES ME HIGH

When I praise you it makes me high
And I feel like I can fly
Up to heaven where they praise you constantly
No drug could ever compare
To the love that we both share
When I praise you I don't have a care

PASTOR I'M SO THANKFUL FOR YOUR LOVE

Pastor I'm so thankful for your love
Sent down from the Father above
Through your words I can tell that it's true love
As you pray for me, in my spirit I become free
And I will thank you throughout all eternity

I LAY ME DOWN TO SLEEP

I lay me down to sleep
I awakened for the Lord sustained me
I lay me down to sleep
I awakened for the Lord sustained me
So whom shall I fear
So whom shall I be afraid of
I lay me down to sleep
I awakened for the Lord sustained me

MY SPIRIT LIVES INSIDE OF YOU

My spirit lives inside of you
He will truly lead and guide you
He will lead you into a life away from sin so you can win

AS THE RAIN COMES FROM THE SKY

As the rain comes from the sky
Think of my love between you and I
It's sweeter than pumpkin pie

I HAVE THE NATURE OF MY FATHER

I Have the nature of my Father
I am the clay and He's my potter
He molds and makes me
Into what He wants me to be
I have the nature of my Father
I am Maryann His daughter

AIN'T GOING TO LET NO ROCKS CRY FOR ME

Ain't going to let no rocks cry for me
Ain't going to let no rock cry for me yea
When I feel like pouting I'll just start to shouting
Ain't going to let no rocks cry for me

Ain't going to let no rocks give up my praise
Ain't going to let no rocks give up my praise yea
When I feel like pouting I'll just start to shouting
Ain't going to let no rocks cry for me

HOLY ONE ARE YOU

Holy one are you
Holy one are you
Alpha and Omega
Beginning and the end
Holy one are you

THE SKY IS BLUE

The sky is blue
My love for you is true
Remember when you said I do
You are married to me for eternity
I'll make you happy, happy, yes indeed

DOWN AT THE ALTAR

Down at the altar I said I do
For your love for me is really true
Yes, I gladly will marry you
For your love for me is really true
As I look into your eyes help me to realize
You love me just as I am
For you are the great I Am

BEFORE THE DAWNING OF THE MORNING

Before the dawning of the morning I'll sing a praise to you
Before the dawning of the morning my heart I will renew
Before the dawning of the morning my heart will cry out to you
Before the dawning of the morning I will worship you

I HAVE CALLED MY PEOPLE TO PRAY

I have called my people to pray
I have called my people to pray
I have called my people to pray
For the world has need of you
And I need you too
I have called my people to pray
If you come and pray to me
I will hear your plea
I have called my people to pray

DON'T GIVE UP I'LL SHOW YOU THE WAY

Don't give up I'll show you the way
Don't give up each and every day
Just rise and sing and praise your King
Don't give up just praise and sing
At my feet your praise is sweet
Just stay at my feet and praise and sing

BE ADDICTED TO ME

Be addicted to me I'll set you free
Be addicted to me I'll set you free
I died on the cross to save your soul
Be addicted to me I'll make you whole
An addiction is a strong hold
But through me you can overcome
An addiction is a strong hold
But through me you can overcome
Be addicted to me I'll set you free

THE DEVIL WAS DEFEATED

The devil was defeated through the blood of the lamb
The devil was defeated by the great I Am
The devil was defeated on the Cross at Calvary
Hallelujah, hallelujah, Jesus won the victory
Hallelujah, hallelujah, He gave His life for you and me

PART TWO: PRAYER SONGS

KEEP ME LORD

Keep me Lord
Keep me Lord
Help me not be ashamed
For my trust and my refuge are in you
Keep me Lord
Keep me Lord
Help me not be ashamed
For my trust and refuge are in you

OH JESUS I NEED YOU TO COMFORT ME

Oh Jesus I need you to comfort me
Oh Jesus I need you to comfort me
Take this pain inside of my heart
And feel it with peace
Oh Jesus I need you
Oh Jesus I need you
Oh Jesus I need you to comfort me

HELP ME BE PLEASING IN YOUR SIGHT

Once again help me be pleasing in your sight
Once again deliver us from our sins
Once again help me be pleasing in your sight
Once again Lord, once again

HEAL ME LORD AND I WILL BE HEALED

Heal me Lord and I will be healed
Save me oh Lord and I will be saved
For you are the one that I praise
For you are the one that I praise
Heal me, save me
Heal me, save me
For you are the one that I praise
For you are the one that I praise

OH LORD PLEASE FORGIVE ME
FOR TAKING MY EYES OFF OF YOU

Oh Lord please forgive me for taking my eyes off of you
Oh Lord please forgive me for taking my eyes off of you
I have tried to do things my way instead of trusting you
Oh Lord please forgive me for taking my eyes off you
Help me look to you once again
You are my closest friend
Oh Lord please forgive me for taking my eyes off of you

PART THREE: TRINITY SONGS

NO MATTER WHAT I'M GOING THROUGH GOD WILL MAKE A WAY

No matter what I'm going through God will make a way
No matter what I'm going through God will make a way
In the middle of my morning, in the middle of my day
When my night seems dark and gloomy I can lift my voice and say
No matter what I'm going through God will make a way
No matter what I'm going through God will make a way

EVERYTHING THAT GOD MADE IT WAS VERY GOOD

Everything that God made it was very good
Everything that God made it was very good
It was good for Paul and Silas
And it is good for me and you
Oh everything that God made it was very good

It was good yea, it was very good
It was good yea, it was very good
It was good for Paul and Silas
And it is good for me and you
Oh everything that God made it was very good

WHEN IT COMES TO GOD'S ANOINTING THERE'S NO AGE

When it comes to God's anointing there's no age
When it comes to God's anointing there's no age
Out of the mouth of babes
He perfected praise
When it comes to God's anointing there's no age
Don't let age stop you
Get up and give Him praise
When it comes to God's anointing
When it comes to God's anointing
When it comes to God's anointing there's no age

GO TO THE THRONE INSTEAD OF THE PHONE

When you're in trouble don't go to the phone
Go to the throne
Go to the throne
When you're in trouble don't go to the phone
Go to the throne of God

When you need healing stand on the word
Stand on the word
Stand on the word
When you need healing stand on the word
Stand on the word of God

When you want joy sing praises to God
Sing praises to God
Sing praises to God
When you want joy sing praises to God
The joy of the Lord is our strength

IN GOD WILL I BOAST

In God will I boast
In God will I boast
In God will I boast forever

I will lift my voice and sing
I will praise His holy name
In God will I boast forever

I will glorify His name
I will glorify His name
In God will I boast forever

LET GO AND LET GOD HANDLE IT

Let go and let God handle it
He is the source of all your supply
Let go and let God handle it
On Him you can only rely
He loves you unconditionally
And He's always by your side
Let go and let God handle it
He's the source of all your supply

I SING AND PRAY TO GOD

I sing and pray to God
I sing and pray to God
I sing and pray to God yes He is holy
He is the giver of life
He is the giver of life
I sing and pray to God yes He is holy
He is the shelter in the middle of my storm
He is the shelter in the middle of my storm
I sing and pray to God yes He is holy

I WILL CALL UPON MY GOD AND HE WILL HEAR ME

I will call upon my God and He will hear me
I will call upon my God and He will hear me
In the morning, noon, or night I will lift my voice on high
I will call upon my God and He will hear me
Morning noon or night
Morning noon or night
In the morning noon or night I will lift my voice on high
I will call upon my God and He will hear me

I'M GOING TO PRAISE
YOU GOD THROUGH MY PAIN

I'm going to praise you God through my pain
I'm going to praise you God through my pain
When life gets too heavy for me and I feel bound instead of free
I'm going to praise you God through my pain
You have brought me through so much
And I can feel your tender touch
You have brought me through so much
And I can feel your tender touch
I'm going to praise you God through my pain every day
I'm going to praise you God through my pain

I LOVE YOU GOD

I love you God because you have been so good to me
In the middle of my drought and in the times of prosperity
You are my source of supply
I must only trust in thee
I love you God because you have been so good to me
God you have been so good to me
God you have been so good to me
God you have been so good to me
You have been so good to me

THANK YOU SWEET JESUS

Thank you sweet Jesus
Thank you sweet Jesus
Thank you sweet Jesus for dying on the cross for me
Your love is unconditional
Your love is unconditional
Your love is unconditional
Thank you for dying on the cross for me
I surrender my life to you
I surrender my life to you
I surrender my life to you
Thank you for dying on the cross for me

BE A LIGHT FOR JESUS IN THIS WORLD

Be a light for Jesus in this world
Be a light for Jesus in this world
The world is full of darkness so we must be a light
Be a light for Jesus
Be a light for Jesus
Be a light for Jesus in this world

I'M NOT IN A COCOON ANYMORE

I'm not in a cocoon anymore, I'm a butterfly
When I listened to the devil he always made me cry
Now I listen to Jesus my savior
And there is more happiness in my life
I'm not in a cocoon anymore, I'm a butterfly

I'M RISING UP ON THE INSIDE

I'm rising up on the inside through Jesus Christ in me
I'm rising up on the inside through Jesus Christ in me
I don't have any more insecurities because of Jesus Christ in me
Satan had me bound but Jesus set me free
I'm rising up on the inside through Jesus Christ in me
Get back Satan I am free
Get back Satan I am free
Get back Satan I am free
I'm rising up on the inside through Jesus Christ in me

HAVE A GREAT DAY IN THE NAME OF JESUS

Have a great day in the name of Jesus
Have a great day in the name of the Lord
Have a great day in the name of Jesus
Have a great day in the name of the Lord

Jesus is our Savior
He died to set us free
He shed His blood on Calvary
And through His blood we are redeemed

Have a great day in the name of Jesus
Have a great day in the name of the Lord
Have a great day in the name of Jesus
Have a great day in the name of the Lord

There's nobody like my Savior
There's nobody like my King
There's nobody like my Lord of Lords
Yes, Jesus is the real thing
Yes, Jesus is the King of kings

Have a great day in the name of Jesus
Have a great day in the name of the Lord
Have a great day in the name of Jesus
Have a great day in the name of the Lord

GET UP OUT OF YOUR SEATS AND PRAISE WITH ME

Get up out of your seats and praise with me
Get up out of your seats and praise with me
Get up out of your seats and praise with me
Give praise to the King, to the King of kings

Get up out of your seats and praise with me
Get up out of your seats and praise with me
Get up out of your seats and praise with me
Give praise to the King, to the King of kings

His name is Jesus
Give Him praise
Give Him praise
Give Him praise all day
His name is Jesus, give praise to the King of kings

He woke me up this morning started me on my way
Put food on my table now I am blessed to say
Get up out of your seats and praise with me
Get up out of your seats and praise with me
Get up out of your seats and praise with me
Give praise to the King of kings

WHATEVER YOUR WILL IS, LORD I SURRENDER

Whatever your will is, Lord I surrender
Whatever your will is, Lord I yield
Whatever your will is, Lord I surrender
Whatever your will is, Lord I yield

I bow before your presence
And I surrender my own will
I bow before your presence
And I surrender my own will

Whatever your will is, Lord I surrender
Whatever your will is, Lord I yield

MY SONGS WILL PRAISE YOU EVERY DAY

My songs will praise you every day
My songs will praise you every day
I love you Jesus more than words can say
My songs will praise you
My songs will praise you
My songs will praise you every day

NEVER GET TOO BUSY FOR JESUS

Never get too busy for Jesus
Always make time for Him
He paid a painful price to free us from our sins
He loves us unconditionally
He wants to be our closest friend

Never get too busy for Jesus
Always make time for Him
He's the Lilly of the Valley
He's the bright and morning star
Never get too busy for Jesus
Always make time for Him

GOOD MORNING JESUS
GOOD MORNING LORD

Good morning Jesus, good morning Lord
Good morning Jesus, good morning Lord
You are my King of kings you are my Lord
Good morning Jesus, good Morning Lord

Thank you for dying for me
Thank you for setting me free
Good morning Jesus, good Morning Lord
I will seek you while you may be found
You're the only real help around
Good morning Jesus, good morning Lord

JESUS I LOVE YOU, PRAISE YOU, AND NEED YOU

Jesus I love you
Jesus I love you
Jesus I love you yes I do
Jesus I praise you
Jesus I praise you
Jesus I praise you yes I do
Jesus I need you
Jesus I need you
Jesus I need you yes I do

MUM JESUS IS SO GOOD

Mum Jesus is so good
Mum Jesus is so good
You can love Him in the morning
You can love Him in the night
Jesus is always on my mind

Mum Jesus is so good
Mum Jesus is so good
He's closer than a brother and He really loves me
I will love Him throughout all eternity
Mum Jesus is so good
Mum Jesus is so good

DON'T STOP, GET UP AND PRAISE HIM

Don't stop, get up and praise Him
Don't stop, get up and praise Him
Don't stop, get up and praise Him Jesus yea
Don't stop, get up and praise Him
Don't stop, get up and praise Him
Don't stop, get up and praise Him Jesus yea

I BELIEVE THAT JESUS DIED FOR ME

I believe that Jesus died for me
He shed His blood on the Cross at Calvary
By His stripes I am healed yes indeed

I believe
I believe
I believe

I believe that Jesus died for me
He shed His blood on the Cross at Calvary
By His stripes I am healed yes indeed

I believe
I believe
I believe

MY BEST FRIEND IS JESUS

My best friend is Jesus
He loves you and me
My best friend is Jesus
He died to set us free
Though my sins were too many, too many to count
He paid the price for me
My best friend is Jesus
He loves you and me

YOU'RE NOT ALONE, JESUS IS WITH YOU

You're not alone Jesus is with you
You're not alone Jesus cares
You're not alone Jesus is with you
You're not alone Jesus cares
When it seems like no one cares
All along He is right there
You're not alone Jesus is with you
You're not alone Jesus cares

JESUS IS WORTHY OF MY PRAISE

Jesus is worthy of my praise
Jesus is worthy of my praise
He paid the price for my life
Jesus is worthy of my praise

Jesus is worthy of my praise
Jesus is worthy of my praise
He paid the price for my life
Jesus is worthy of my praise

He's worthy
He's worthy
Jesus is worthy of my praise
He's worthy
He's worthy
Jesus is worthy of my praise

HOLY SPIRIT, MY COMFORTER I NEED YOU

Holy Spirit, my comforter I need you
You are here by my side to be my guide
Holy Spirit, my comforter I need you
In the morning I need you
In the afternoon I need you too
In the dark and gloomy night
I need you to be my guide
Holy Spirit, my comforter I need you
Holy Spirit, my comforter
Holy Spirit, my comforter
Holy Spirit, my comforter I need you

LEAD ME HOLY SPIRIT

Lead me Holy Spirit
Lead me today
Lead me Holy Spirit
Please show me the way
Lead me Holy Spirit
Lead me today
Lead me Holy Spirit
Please show me the way
Lead me and guide me into truth
Lead me this very day
Holy Spirit, my comforter I need you
Thank you for showing me the way

PART FOUR: SONGS OF DECLARATION & ANTICIPATION

WE'RE IN THE ARMY OF THE LORD

We're in the army, the army of the Lord
So we must fight, fight, fight, until we get it right
We're in the army, the army of the Lord
So we must fight, fight, fight, until we get it right

We don't fight in a fleshly way
We put on the armor God's way
We're in the army, the army of the Lord
So we must fight, fight, fight, until we get it right

Fight the devil with God's word
Fight the devil with God's word
We're in the army, the army of the Lord
So we must fight, fight, fight, until we get it right

We're in the army, the army of the Lord
So we must fight, fight, fight, until we get it right

ALL THINGS WORK TOGETHER FOR OUR GOOD

All things work together for our good
All things work together for our good
According to His promises for our good
All things work together
All things work together
All things work together for our good

IT'S TIME FOR OUR LIGHT TO SHINE

It's time for our light to shine
It's time for our light to shine
Many people are dying
Because the devil has blinded their eyes
We must show them the truth about how to live their lives
It's time for our light to shine
It's time for our light to shine

People are in so much pain they look for drugs as an escape
We must share the love of Jesus everywhere,
So people will know that He cares
It's time for our light to shine
It's time for our light to shine

I'M EXPECTING GREAT THINGS TO COME MY WAY

I'm expecting great things to come my way
I'm expecting great things each and every day
From the north, south, east, and west
Great things are coming my way
I'm expecting great things to come my way
Angles go and get my blessing
And bring them to me this very day
Angles go and get my blessings
And bring them to me this very day

I'M A NEW CREATION IN THE LORD

I'm a new creation in the Lord
I'm a new creation in the Lord
Old things have passed away
All things are new
Jesus forgave me of my sins
And through Him I'm born again
I'm a new creation in the Lord
The old me is gone, the new me carries on
I'm a new creation in the Lord

MY FAMILY IS SAVED AND THEY'RE FILLED WITH THE HOLY GHOST

My family is saved and they're filled with the Holy Ghost
My family is saved and they're filled with the Holy Ghost
Baptized and filled with Him, and yes they're born again
My family is saved and they're filled with the Holy Ghost
We confess what we believe in our heart
We confess what we believe in our heart
My family is saved and they're filled with the Holy Ghost
My family is saved and they're filled with the Holy Ghost

WHAT GREAT THINGS ARE GOING TO HAPPEN TODAY FOR ME

What great things are going to happen today for me
What great things are going to happen today for me
I don't look to the left, I don't look to the right
My faith is in Jesus Christ

What great things are going to happen today for me?
Every day is a new beginning through Jesus Christ my Lord
Every day is a new beginning through Jesus Christ my Lord
What great things are going to happen today for me

PART FIVE: MEMORY POEMS OF MY MOM PATRICIA

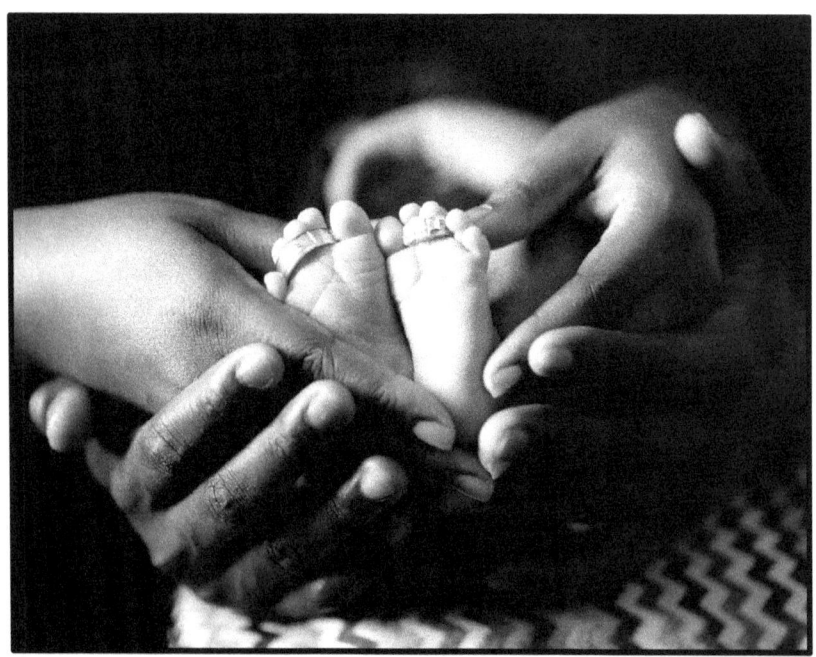

<u>MOM TAUGHT ME HOW TO WORK</u>

Mom taught me how to work you see
She had two jobs for many years
How she was an example to me
She worked hard to take care of us
It was not an easy job but it was a must
So thank you Mom for all you did
You kept me alive and allowed me to live
You taught me through the years to hang in there
Because quitters never win
And winners never quit
Oh Mom, you were such a great example to me
I will hold on to these great memories

MOM CRIED ON MY GRADUATION DAY

Oh what a day for her to see her daughter Maryann graduating
That was her dream
I got pregnant at seventeen
It seemed like my mom's dream had come to an end
Oh I was so ashamed I broke my mom's heart and caused her pain
What could I do to make things right again
So I chose to stay in school
I just had to help my mom's dream come true
So nine months pregnant I walked across the stage
My mom was so happy to see that day
It wasn't easy being pregnant in school
But I had to help my mom's dream come true
Oh how my mom cried with joy that day
Her daughter made it through school, hey, hey, hey

I MISS MY MOM, YES I DO

I miss my mom, yes I do
If your mom is gone I'm sure you miss her too
My mom went through a lot before she had me
She could have chosen to give me away
But I believe God spoke to her heart and said, let her stay
You see God had a purpose for me all along
He knew that I would write many poems and sing many songs
I miss you, Momma, yes I do
Now you're with Jesus and I'm happy for you

MOMMA'S CHRISTMAS BOXES

Momma gave Christmas boxes to me and my family
She filled them with food and plenty of toiletries
Momma knew how to plan ahead
At times when we were low and needed some food
She would send some over like I knew she would
Momma I will always remember you
And your wonderful Christmas boxes too

MOMMA PRESSED MY HAIR

Momma pressed my hair, oh it was so much pain
I was a tender headed little girl, oh what a shame
I remember when she told me to hold back my ear
I thought, wow she's going to burn me because the heat was so near
Oh but when Momma got done with my hair
I wanted to show it off everywhere

MOM HAD A SPECIAL HEART

Mom took care of people for a living
She had a special heart that kept on giving
She took care of people at the nursing home
She loved them like they were her very own

MOMMA'S PERFUME

Momma had such good taste when she wore her perfume
I knew she was around, I could smell her in the room
Whenever I smell that scent on someone oh how I think of you
Momma had such good taste and she always smelled so good

MY MOM WAS A GOOD COOK

My mom had a special way of cooking her food
Many times she made concoctions and they were really good
She mixed a little bit of this and a little bit of that
It always turned out good as a matter of fact
Her chili and her spaghetti were two of my favorite things
And those pinto beans and ham hocks were also good
She really did her thing
No one can cook like my mom, she was one of a kind
These are kind thoughts coming from my mind

MOM MADE ME EAT LIVER

Mom made me eat liver this is true
I didn't like it but I did what she told me to do
She said eat it because it's good for you
She only did what moms are supposed to do

MOMMA'S SPECIAL NIGHT

It was Momma's special night
Oh she looked so good
She was dressed in her pretty flowered dress
And oh she smelled so good
The limousine pulled up and picked us both up
We had a special time together
And the memories were good
She was dressed in her pretty flowered dress
And oh she smelled so good

MOM LOVED TO HEAR ME SING

Mom loved to hear me sing
And I loved to sing for her too
I sang on special occasions like Christmas and birthdays too
One day I sang to my mom and she began to cry
She got up and went in the other room so she could wipe her eyes
Sometimes crying cleanses the heart
And also crying can help you have a brand new start

MOMMA'S WIGS

Momma wore such pretty wigs they looked so pretty on her
Her hair was full of bouncy, bouncy, bouncy, beautiful curls
I look so much like my mom, yes I really do
It amazing the reflection that I see
When I look in the mirror, I see you and me

THANK YOU MOM FOR HAVING ME

Thank you Mom for having me
When you went through so much abuse
I'm sure every time you looked at me
You remembered what you went through
You chose to love me anyway in spite of your memory of pain
Now I go forward in what God has for me to do
And I will always be thankful that God delivered me through you

MOM TOOK CARE OF ME WHEN I WAS SICK

When I was sick my mom would rub my chest with Vicks
Then she gave me a hot toddy so I could rest
Mom always had a way to make me feel better
She knew what to do no matter what the weather

MY MOM KEPT ME IN A DRESSER DRAWER

My mom kept me safe in a dresser drawer
My bed wasn't secure enough I could have fallen on the floor
I was her three pound baby that she adored
I was so beautiful she couldn't ask for anything more

HIGH HEEL SHOES

When I was a little girl I liked to walk in my mom's high heel shoes
The heels were high and they were pretty too
I would put them on my feet and walk a little way
Then I would fall down again and again
What a great memory of my mom's shoes
I was just doing things that girls like to do

MOMMA'S JEAN SKIRTS AND TOPS

Momma loved her jean skirts
And she loved her jean tops too
She got them at family dollar at a good price too
Mom looked for specials for herself and for us too
She knew how to plan ahead
That was a very smart thing for her to do
Momma I also look for specials
I learned that from you

MOMMA DIDN'T LIKE ROSES

Momma didn't like roses because they died too fast
Instead I gave her chocolate ones
And surrounded them with cash
My mom's face lit up like a Christmas tree
And she gave me a big hug
I felt so good inside to show my mother love

MOMMA TRIED TO WARN ME
TO TAKE CARE OF MY FEET

Momma tried to warn me to take care of my feet
She had 2 pair of shoes for work and she changed them every day
So her feet would stay dry and wouldn't be stinky
Later in life her feet begin to ache
Then they began to throb because she had two jobs
Now years later I remember what she said
Sometimes my feet hurt so bad I want to stay in bed

MOM'S WORDS OF WISDOM
RINGING THROUGH MY EARS

Mom's words of wisdom are ringing through my ears
Many things that she told me I didn't always want to hear
Now that I'm older and my mom is gone away
Her words of wisdom come to me again and again

MOMMA GAVE ME BEAUTIFUL CARDS

Momma gave me beautiful cards
Her penmanship was nice
I didn't only read them once
I often read them twice

MOMMA HAD A GREEN THUMB

Momma had a green thumb she really loved her plants
She loved her purple passions and that was a fact
She had plant hangers in the corner of the living room
The sun shined brightly on them and they began to bloom

MOMMA'S GRAY CAT SMOKEY

Momma's gray cat Smokey was her very special cat
She loved her cat very much and that was a fact
He knew when she was gone
And he knew when she came home too
Smokey had a special place in Momma's bed
He didn't like to share his space
If you tried to move him he would bite or scratch your hand
So Momma had to pick him up and put him on the floor
Smokey looked at Mom with disgust on his face
He didn't want to move
He didn't want anyone to take his place

I MADE A SONG FOR MY MOM

I made a song for my mom before she passed away
She was ready to go into the arms of Jesus
She didn't want to stay
I held her in my arms
And sang the song to her
Soon it got too late and I couldn't seem to stay awake
My sister woke me up and said that Mom was gone
And I began to weep
Knowing that Mom received Jesus again
That gave me great peace within
She's gone for now, but one day I will see her again

I LOVE YOU MOMMA

I love you Momma, I love you so much
I love you Momma, you taught me so much
Through the years that we shared
You showed me that you cared
I love you Momma, I love you so much
When I was sad you made me so glad
I love you Momma, I love you so much
Even when you depart
I'll keep you in my heart
I love you Momma, I love you so much

PART SIX: POEMS FOR MY DAD

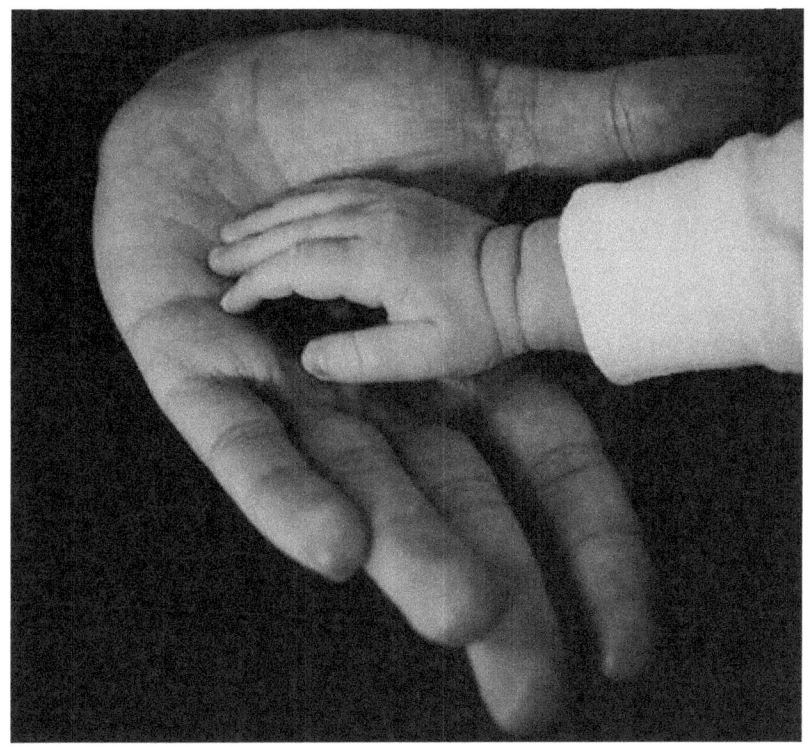

I FORGIVE YOU DADDY FOR NOT BEING THERE

I forgive you Daddy for not being there for me
Many times I even wondered if you cared about me
However the more I come to see you
I feel much father's love from you
You spoke words of life to me
That will forever be in my memory
I forgive you Daddy yes I do
And always remember that Jesus loves you
And I love you too

I LOVE YOU DADDY

I love you Daddy yes I do
I wouldn't be in the world without you
I know if you weren't in jail you would be here with me
I forgive you and I pray the best for you
And always remember that Jesus loves you

MEMORIES WITH MY DAD

I remember when I was a little girl
And I got to come and see you
You would pick me up and hold me in your arms
Like daddies often do
Oh I felt so safe when I was with you
No one could hurt me then
They would have to come past you

PART SEVEN:
FEATURED GUEST
MY BOSS, CHERYL CROSS

My boss Cheryl Cross is a beautiful Italian lady. She has six wonderful children like the Brady Bunch: Three beautiful daughters, three handsome sons, and three beautiful grandkids that she also loves very much.

For 10 years I have been blessed to have her as a boss at House of Mercy. Cheryl came to work at House of Mercy in 2006. Combined with her work at Mercy Hospital and House of Mercy, it has been 30 years.

At Mercy Hospital many of those years were spent in food service. Cheryl has a lot of wisdom when it comes to nutrition. She brought color to the salad bar with many fresh fruits and veggies. She is just colorful in every way, from the food that she prepares to the colorful clothes that she wears. She knows how to whet the women and children's appetite by spreading an array of yummy delights.

Here, in my book, she is holding a tray of yummy treats that she ordered especially for the ladies and children for the holiday. The ladies and children love her so much and they look forward to her yummy hot breakfast on Mondays, Thursdays, and Sundays—and when she works the holidays too.

Though she is small in size, she's a giant on the inside. She will stand up for what she believes in and she's not afraid of any bully. She cares about her staff, and whenever she needs to, she will stand up on our behalf. I can see why God blessed her with so many kids. She loves them and she's a great example to them.

She loves Jesus and I love Jesus too—that's a special bond between us. We laugh together and cry together too, that's a thing that friends usually do. For our birthdays she spoils us and we spoil her too, because we love each other, we really do. We both like gospel music and some oldies too. She will soon be 54, it is really hard to believe. She's so beautiful, she could pass for 33. Here's a song I wrote for her not long after she first started at House of Mercy.

CHERYL'S SONG

What a blessing you have been
Since you came to the House of Mercy
God's love is felt through you
In so many ways you brought life to things that were dead
And brought color to things that were colorless
I'm so glad that you are here, that you are here, that you are here

FUN DAY MONDAY

Another amazing thing about Cheryl is a thing she does called *Fun Day Monday* where she gets together with her kids and they have fun. Her grandkids love to come to Grandma's house and have fun too. Cheryl is such a fun-loving lady. She has amazing hairstyles, cute clothes, and cute boots. Thank you, Cheryl, for allowing God's love and compassion to flow through you, and always remember that Jesus loves you.

PART EIGHT: WORK COMMUNITY

THERE WAS ONCE A GIRL WHO SMELLED SO GOOD

There once was a girl who smelled so good
I could smell her coming yes I could
My nose gets happy whenever she's around
She makes me smile and never frown

God blessed me with a sense of smell
Oh how she wears that oil very well
Oh how you inspired me to write
Whenever you're around my senses come to a new height
There once was a girl who smelled so good
I could smell her coming yes I could

DON'T GIVE UP ON YOUR DREAMS

You have a dream to write
Sometimes you seem a little uptight
The things that you're thinking about, write them down
Soon your memory will come back around
If you have dreams in your heart
You have to work on them daily so they won't depart
Don't give up on yourself
Inside of you is a lot of wealth
You're beautiful this is true
And always remember that Jesus loves you

SOMETIMES WE FEEL LIKE OUR KIDS DRIVE US CRAZY

Sometimes we feel like our kids drive us crazy
But one day they will grow up
And we will wish they were still babies
So cherish the crazy times that you have with them
Because as they get older you will only see them now and then

RED SUIT SUPERVISOR

You look good in every outfit that you wear
But your red suit is my favorite I declare
You have an important job and I pray strength for you
You can do it, just keep your positive attitude
And always remember that Jesus loves you

RC OF MANY HAIRSTYLES

I love your pretty face and your hairstyles too
No matter which way you wear your hair
All of your styles look beautiful on you
You have a very contagious smile
Which blesses everyone around you
I appreciate you and I'm sure many others do too
And always remember that Jesus loves you

PURPLE AND PINK

I saw a lady last week
She was dressed in purple and pink
I told her I liked her colors
She is such a beautiful mother

She is not just cute on the outside
But the inside too
She is very special to me
And I am special to her too
Purple and pink, keep on looking cute like you do
And always remember that Jesus loves you

BATMAN TOP AND BOTTOM

I saw a little boy the other day
He is very handsome I must say
He learned how to spell his name
So he told me over and over again
I told him I was going to put him in a book
Not his name but a made up name: Batman top and shorts

Then he asked me about my apron
I told him, I wash a lot of dishes
And he said, I will help you
Then I laughed with his mom and said,
You are not old enough to help me

Then he gave me a hug and went on his way
We had a great conversation that day
Batman top and shorts, keep on looking cool like you do
And thanks for the hug I received from you
And always remember that Jesus loves you

BLACK LACE SHINGLE DRESS

I was walking down the hall the other day
When a beautiful lady came my way
She had a black lace shingle dress on
It was so amazing and her hair was also beautiful and long
Whenever I see her she always has a big smile on her face
I believe she is very happy to be in her work place
Another day she had on a colorful jacket
It looked so cute I wanted to have one like that too
Black lace shingle dress, keep on looking beautiful like you do
And always remember that Jesus loves you

MINNIE MOUSE POLKA DOT OUTFIT

I saw a pretty little girl today
She had on a Minnie Mouse polka dot outfit
Oh she was looking so cute
On top of that she had beautiful curly hair too
Her mommy always dresses her so cute
Minnie Mouse polka dot outfit, keep on looking cute like you do
And always remember that Jesus loves you

SAME BEAUTIFUL FACE

I met a lady last year, she was very beautiful with long black hair
I hadn't seen her for a while then one day I saw her again
She was still as pretty as she was back then
She always has a smile when we look face to face
I believe that she is really thankful to be in this place
Same beautiful face, keep on looking beautiful like you do
And always remember that Jesus loves you

THERE IS A LADY WHO IS VERY VERY KIND

There is a lady who is very, very kind
She always thanks us for her food
And hugs us from time to time
She is very pretty and she has a great personality too
God bless you, God bless you

BLUE EYES AND BLING BLING WATCH

I met a new lady today
She is very beautiful I must say
She came to the window to get some food
I could tell that she was in a pretty good mood
She had some of the most beautiful eyes that I have ever seen
And she had on a colorful bling bling watch
I thought, you go girl, do your thing
Blue eyes and bling bling watch
Keep on looking beautiful like you do
And always remember that Jesus loves you

AMERICAN FLAG T-SHIRT

I saw a lady that I have known for a while
She always seems to greet me with a beautiful smile
Recently she put a fluff to her hair
Oh it is so beautiful I declare
Then she had on an American flag T-shirt
With the beautiful colors of red, white, and blue
I thought, you go girl
Keep on representing our country like you do
And always remember that Jesus loves you

TANK TOP TUTU DRESS

I saw a little girl the other day
She is very beautiful I must say
She had on a tank top tutu dress
It was very unique I must confess
I told her that she looked so cute
Then she turned around in her little cute tutu
She had a beautiful smile on her face
She knew she was one of the prettiest girls in this place
Tank top tutu dress, keep on looking cute like you do
And always remember that Jesus loves you

STRAWBERRY ICE CREAM

You're a beautiful young lady and you dress really cute too
I thought you looked like a model the day I first met you
You were so excited the day you got your strawberry ice cream
You were like a kid and I was so excited for you
So instead of giving you one scoop I decided to give you two
I enjoy seeing you every day
Your smiling face just makes my day
Strawberry ice cream, I appreciate the kindness I receive from you
And always remember that Jesus loves you

DISNEYLAND PEN

*One of my friends went to Disneyland
For a vacation to spend time with her family
While she was there she decided to think about me
She brought me back a beautiful Minnie Mouse pen
It was in a beautiful case
The top part was a pen and the bottom part was the holder
It made me feel like a happy little kid even though I am older
Disneyland pen, thank you for thinking about me
You made me happy yes indeed
Every time I use my pen I will think about you
And always remember that Jesus loves you*

FAMOUS NAME

*I met a lady a while ago
She is very beautiful don't you know
One thing that is very special about her
Is she was named after a famous cartoon character
And she also has a memory tattoo of her dad on her arm
Which gives her good memories to think on
She has some of the most beautiful hazel colored eyes
And she has a smile as sweet as cool whip on top of pumpkin pie
Famous name, you're a sweetheart this is true
And always remember that Jesus loves you*

RC WITH A SHAG

*I met a RC some time ago, she was very beautiful don't you know
She had a beautiful shag hairdo, it laid to the side, it was pretty
cool She also had a pretty face and a great personality too
Pretty RC with a shag, keep on looking beautiful like you do
And always remember that Jesus loves you*

SUMMER GEM DRESS

*I saw a lady walking down the hallway today
She had a beautiful summer gem dress on, hey, hey, hey
It was bright and yellow like the sunshine in the sky
With beautiful gems and other colorful designs
Summer gem dress, keep on looking beautiful like you do
And always remember that Jesus loves you*

AMERICAN FLAG FINGERNAIL POLISH

*I was in the window serving food the other day
When a beautiful lady came my way
Then I just happened to look down at her hands
She had red white and blue polish on just like the American flag
Wow her fingernail polish really encouraged me
It reminded me of the price that freedom was paid for you and me
American flag fingernail polish
Keep on representing the American flag like you do
And always remember that Jesus loves you*

STAR HOODIE

*I was in the window serving the other day
When a beautiful lady came my way
She had on a gray hoodie full of stars
I thought that is so cute the stars represent who you are
I love to see you every day
You shine like a star in so many ways
Star hoodie, keep on shinning like you do
And always remember that Jesus loves you*

★ ★ ★ ★ ★ ★

YOU'RE A BEAUTIFUL QUEEN

You're a beautiful queen and your children are beautiful too
Oh yes, oh yes, they are a reflection of you
I remember the day when they came to be with you again
You were so happy it showed on your face
Oh how you hugged your children with your motherly embrace
God blessed you to be with them again
Through Jesus Christ we always win

WHEN I LOOK IN THE WINDOW WHO DO I SEE

When I look in the window who do I see?
A beautiful blonde hair girl looking back at me
And oh how I love her beautiful blue eyes
And her smile is like a ray of sunshine
You are so pretty, pretty as can be
God gave you a beautiful face
I'm sure that anyone who sees you loves to embrace
When I look in window who do I see?
A beautiful blonde hair girl looking back at me

THE TWO RED HEADS

The two red heads: mom and son
She is beautiful and he's the handsome one
They both are happy, happy as can be
When I see them smile it makes me very happy
God created you both with pretty red hair
And a beautiful bright smile to share everywhere

I WAS WALKING DOWN THE HALL TODAY

I was walking down the hallway today
When I saw two beautiful women walking my way
And to my surprise what did I hear?
They were singing a Christmas song in Spanish with cheer
Their voices sounded like angles from above
As I listened to them sing oh how I felt God's love

THE OTHER DAY I SAW A LITTLE BABY

The other day I saw a little baby
All bundled up in her mother's arms
Such joy, such joy, such joy filled my heart
I thought, God You're so amazing for giving us such precious gifts
Every day we should praise You with our heart, not just our lips
The other day I saw a little baby
All bundled up in her mother's arms
Such joy, such joy, such joy filled my heart

A BEAUTIFUL LADY EATING WITH HER KIDS

I saw a beautiful lady eating with her kids
They all look so sweet and innocent
You could tell that she really cared about them
They smiled at her and she smiled at them
She was very glad that they were all together again
Miracles happen every day
I'm glad that God brought one your way
You are beautiful this is true
And always remember that Jesus loves you

A REFLECTION OF MY NIECE

You look like my niece, yes, she is beautiful like you
You both have pretty hair and pretty face
And a great personality too
You always make me smile whenever I see you
And the love you have for your son is very precious too
Yes, you're a reflection of my niece
I see her whenever I look at you
You have a gift of poetry
This is a gift that God has given to you
Use your gift to be a blessing
And somehow it will come back to you
And always remember that Jesus loves you

SHE'S SUCH A PRETTY LITTLE GIRL

She's such a pretty little girl
Oh how she use to be so shy
Now she smiles at me
And sometimes tells me hi
Her mom is also beautiful and she talks to me a lot too
Whenever I see them I always have good thoughts
I feel God's love through both of you
And I am always happy to see you two

THE GIRL WITH WAVY HAIR

As I walked down the hallway what who did I see?
A girl with wavy hair in front of me
I thought, wow she is beautiful, this is true,
And I love her wavy hair, yes I do

YOU'RE SUCH A BEAUTIFUL LADY

You are such a beautiful lady
And your daughter is very beautiful too
I will miss you and your daughter
And your funny personality too
God bless you and your daughter too
I pray great things work out for you
You are a beautiful lady
And your daughter is very beautiful too

I APPRECIATE THE KIND WORDS

I appreciate the kind words that I received from you
Especially when you told me you appreciate everything I do
You're a wonderful mom and you have a great personality too
Anyone would be glad to have such a wonderful friend like you
God gave you such a kind heart I see it every day
I will always remember you when you're near or far away

YOU ARE STILL AS BEAUTIFUL AS YOU WERE YEARS AGO

You are still as beautiful as you were years ago
And your boys are very handsome too
I love your beautiful blonde hair
It really looks good on you
So whenever I see your smiling face
Share that beautiful smile that God gave to you
You are still as beautiful as you were years ago
And your boys are very handsome too

THE LADY WITH THE PRETTY HAIRCUT

The lady with the pretty haircut just walked past me
Wow she was pretty, pretty as can be
She smiled, and smiled, and smiled at me
I could tell that she was happy, happy yes indeed
Then one day she put on her bling bling hat
Then she really looked cool as a matter of fact

THERE IS A LADY WHO KNOWS WHAT WE GO THROUGH

There is a lady who knows what we go through
Because many times she has been in our shoes
She has a lot of compassion for what we do
She knows sometimes we're a busy crew
Many times she's had to work hard too
God bless you lady, I appreciate you
And thank you for the compassion that we receive from you

YOU'RE SUCH A HAPPY LADY

You're such a happy lady
And you're very beautiful too
I appreciate the kindness that I always receive from you
I receive your kindness like a magnet
We all need to have it
God gave you a kind heart I believe this is true
I will always remember that kindness I received from you

I WILL MISS YOU BEAUTIFUL LADY

I will miss you, beautiful lady and your handsome son too
Your son has a special gift, his smiles light up the room
He always likes to smile and call out my name
He made me feel so special when he called out my name
I will miss you, beautiful lady, and your handsome son too
Take care of yourself and your smiley boy too

SOMETIMES YOU SMILE WHEN YOU'RE IN PAIN

Sometimes you smile when you're in pain
Really your smile helps you from going insane
Lift your head up to the sky
Jesus loves you and so do I
If you think of these words that I say to you
They will not only lift you up but encourage you too
My name is Maryann, with songs of inspiration
God is using me to bring healing to the nations

PRETTY DRESS AND COLORFUL JEWELS

She had on a pretty black dress and colorful jewels
And she also had a beautiful smile too
I love her great personality
She is always happy, happy as can be
She's not just pretty she's also cool
She has a kind and gentle heart
I could tell that about her right from the start

WHITE AND GOLD

I saw a little girl in the hallway today
She was dressed in white and gold on a beautiful Christmas day
She looked like a little angel from heaven above
When I saw her smile I felt God's love
Her mom was so happy, happy as can be
To see her little girl looking so pretty

HE'S A HAPPY BABY BOY

He's a happy baby boy
And he is very handsome too
His mom is also happy
And she is very beautiful too
He used to be so shy whenever I talked to him
Now he likes to say hi to me over and over again

HE SANG HAPPY BIRTHDAY IN MY EAR

A little boy wanted to sing happy birthday to me
So I bent down so he could sing it in my ear
My heart was so touched
Inside I cried happy tears
It's amazing how God shows love to me each and every day
To have a kid sing to me is a very special thing

WOMAN OF MANY HATS

She's a woman of many hats don't you know
Every time she turns around she is on the go
I have worked with her for many years
We laughed a lot together and also shed some tears
I have shared thousands of songs from my heart
All because she gave me my first start

THE FAMILY WHO SMILES

I met a beautiful lady with two little boys who always smile at me
They always seem to be so very happy, happy yes indeed
Though sometimes they cry because they are little kids
But then they smile again and again
Because they know their mommy loves both of them

RED SWEATER AND FRENCH BRAIDS

I saw a beautiful lady the other day
She had on my favorite color I just have to say
A beautiful red sweater is what she wore
And her lovely French braids I did adore

THE LADY WITH THE PRETTY BLACK HAIR

The lady sat behind me with pretty black wavy hair
Her smile was so bright you could see it anywhere
Her baby sat beside her in his baby stroller chair
The baby felt at peace because his mommy was right there

QUIET PERSONALITY

She's a beautiful lady with a quiet personality
Whenever she comes to the window she always smiles at me
Today for the first times I saw her pretty long black hair
She is so beautiful I declare

DECEMBER 30TH WAS HER SPECIAL DAY

December 30th was her special day
She was blessed with a bundle of joy, hey, hey, hey
She's the kind of lady who people love to hang around
She always makes me smile and never ever frown
Whenever I see her face
I feel God's warm embrace

MOMMY AND SON

The other day I saw a beautiful lady eating with her son
She spoke to him with a sweet soft voice
Then encouraged him to eat some more
Oh how it touched my heart that day to see a mother's love
She is always so happy whenever she is with her son
Her son is one of a kind, he is her number one

MOTHER AND SON TOGETHER AGAIN

A mother and son together again
Oh I am so excited for them
She was so happy to see him
She hopes never to be separated from him again
Your son is one kind young man
And you are special too
Miracles happen every day
I see one has happened for you

RADIANT SMILE

I like your great personality
And your radiant smile too
But most importantly I love your positive attitude
You're a great example for the women and children
And also for me too
I appreciate the kindness that I always receive from you
God has given you a kind heart
Keep on helping people like you do
And always remember that Jesus loves you

SHE'S A LADY WHO SMILES EVERY DAY

She's a lady who smiles every day
And her voice is as soft as the ocean waves
She has beautiful, beautiful, wavy hair
People come to see her from everywhere
She is always so kind to me
And she always takes time to talk to me
I love her yes I do
And yes she is beautiful too

SHE ALWAYS SAYS HI TO ME

There is a kind lady I know
She always says hi to me
She calls me by my name
That is so very special to me
Thank you for taking time to be so kind to me
I appreciate you
And you appreciate me
God bless you, kind lady
I will always remember you
And I pray that the kindness you give
One day comes back to you

TINY AND SWEET

I met a beautiful lady the other day
She was tiny and sweet I would have to say
She always likes to talk to me
And she has one of the sweetest personalities
She has three kids and they're special too
Her older son always likes to talk to me too

ORANGE AND BLACK HOODIE

She has a beautiful smile and a pretty face
And her black and orange hoodie is off the chain
Her friends love it whenever she's around
She always makes them smile and never frown
She's a one of a kind girl
She's one we all adore
Keep your focus on all that you do
And always remember that Jesus loves you

FROZEN BLUE APRON WITH WHITE SNOWFLAKES

I was in the serving room the other day
When I saw a beautiful little girl in the hallway
She had on a beautiful apron from the movie Frozen
With pretty white snowflakes all over it
Then she started singing the Frozen movie theme song
And she sounded really good
She had some of the most beautiful curly hair
And she had a smile so bright you could see it anywhere
Frozen blue apron with white snowflakes
Keep on looking beautiful like you do
And always remember that Jesus loves you

SO CUTE

Every time I see you, you look so cute
No matter what you wear you have matching boots
On top of that you have a great personality too
You care about us, and we care about you too
God has given you a giving heart
I could tell that about you right from the start

FLIPPED HAIR AND PRETTY EARRINGS

I met a beautiful lady just the other day
She really looked amazing, hey, hey, hey
She had flipped hair
And beautiful earrings that sparkled on her ears
At one time they were her mom's, now they are hers
Whenever she wears them she feels her mother's love

BLONDE HAIR AND RED SWEAT SUIT

I met a girl who is so cute
She has beautiful blonde hair
And a red sweat suit
Her hair was so long it went down her back
I love blonde hair as a matter of fact
She is always so kind to me
I really love her great personality

MOTHER AND SON EATING BREAKFAST

Mother and son eating breakfast together
Staying warm inside because outside is really cold weather
They sat and ate and talked about what to do today
Then they got up and went to finish their day

THE LADY NEXT TO ME

There was a lady sitting next to me
She was so kind and very pretty
Her baby boy was very handsome too
He had a smile as bright as a Christmas tree
Because he loved sitting next to his mommy

GREAT ATTITUDE

You have a great attitude
And you are so amazing to me
I also love your great personality
I really enjoy working with you
You never complain you just do what we want you to do

SHE'S A SNAZZY LADY

She's a snazzy lady
And she is really kind
Yes, she is a friend of mine
She always has a smile for me
And she treats me very respectfully
There are not many like her
She's the kind of lady anyone would adore
She's a snazzy lady and she is one of a kind
Yes, she is a friend of mine

A LITTLE BABY GIRL SINGING TO HER MOM

A little baby girl was singing to her mom
Then she blew her a kiss with her sweet little lips
I thought, oh how adorable to see such a thing
She loved her mommy so much she wanted her to hear her sing
Baby girl, keep on singing to your mommy like you do
And always remember that Jesus loves you

THANK YOU CARD

I came to work a few months ago,
On the table was a card waiting for me,
I opened it up and read it
Oh how it touched my heart to have kind words spoken back to me
I gave a lady a beautiful picture frame poem
That I wrote from my heart
She was so excited about her poem
She responded with a thank you card
Thank you card, keep on being kind and beautiful too
And always remember that Jesus loves you

SHE IS A PRETTY LADY WITH CUTE BOOTS

She is a pretty lady
And her little girl is very pretty too
She has beautiful black hair
And she always wears cute boots
Her little girl smiles sometimes whenever she sees me
And many times she also reaches out her hand to me

BLONDE HAIR AND SPIKED HAIR

She's a beautiful blonde haired lady
And her make up is very beautiful too
She has a new baby girl with spiked hair
Oh she's so beautiful too
She was wrapped up in her pink blanket
As her mom held her in her arms
I thought, oh how precious
They have such a wonderful bond

I LOVE SEEING YOUR SMILING FACE

I love seeing your smiling face
And I think it's very special that we have close birthdays
You are an amazing young lady
And you are very beautiful too
You do such a great job with the teens
And I'm sure they appreciate you too
Keep on doing what you do
I am so glad to have an awesome coworker like you
And always remember that Jesus loves you too

I WILL MISS YOU AND YOUR BABY TOO

I will miss you and your baby too
And also the beautiful smile that I always receive from you
You are blessed with a smile from above
When I see you smile I feel Gods love
I will miss you and your baby too

EYESHADOW

You're very beautiful
And your eyeshadow is beautiful too
No matter what color you wear it all looks good on you
You're an amazing lady and you also have a cute hairdo
On top of all that you're an amazing cook too

YUMMY BANANA BREAD

A beautiful lady came to help in the kitchen one day
She made some yummy to my tummy fantastic banana bread
The aroma filled the air as people sniffed everywhere
I told her to make enough so that there would be plenty to share
I have to admit her bread was a big hit

COWBOY JERSEY AND FRENCH BRAIDS

She had on a cowboy jersey and French braids in her hair
She looked very pretty I do declare
She always has a smile for me
And she also has a great personality
She is a pretty lady inside and out
That's what her poem is all about
Stay focused on all that you do
And always remember that Jesus loves you

ORANGE PURSE AND PRETTY WIG

I said goodbye to a pretty lady today
I gave her a hug and she went on her way
She had on a pretty wig
And she had a beautiful orange purse too
She liked to change her appearance
She always looked fresh and new
Her other poem is called pretty as a picture
Yes it is true

PRETTY AS A PICTURE

Pretty as a picture is what you are to me
When I look at you, beauty is what I see
From your eyelashes and fingernails, to the flowers in your hair
You're pretty as a picture I declare
Every time I see your new hairdo
All I want to do is write about you
Pretty as a picture is what you are to me
Jesus loves you and Jesus loves me

A BEAUTIFUL LADY WITH LONG BLACK HAIR

A beautiful lady with long black hair
Had a precious baby with lots of curls in his hair
She had him dressed in camouflage green
Oh that was so precious to me
She cried because her heart was filled with joy
Because God had blessed her with a precious baby boy

STRAWBERRY BLONDE & CUTE FINGERNAILS

I met a lady the other day
She was very pretty I must say
She has the most beautiful strawberry blonde hair
And the cutest fingernails I declare
She also had a pretty little girl
Who everyone around her adores
When she's with her little girl
She is one of the happiest ladies in the world
Strawberry blonde hair and cute fingernails
Keep on looking cute like you do
And always remember that Jesus loves you

HUGS AND KISSES

I saw something the other day
That really touched my heart
A mommy hugging and kissing her daughter
You could tell she loved her with all of her heart
She smiled at her mommy
And her mommy smiled at her
She was so glad that she was her little girl

MOTHER EATING LUNCH WITH HER CHILDREN

A mother was eating lunch with her children as I began to pray
She told her kids to be quiet in a very respectful way
I appreciate the kindness and the respect that she showed me
She took the time to talk to them
They listened and agreed

They ate and laughed together
You could tell that they were friends
She is a very beautifully young lady
And her kids are beautiful too
I appreciate the kindness and respect I received from you
Stay focused in all that you do
Your precious kids love you and need you too

MOMMY & HER KIDS EATING A SNACK

Mommy and her kids eating a snack
The atmosphere was filled with fresh oranges as a matter of fact
They were out of school enjoying their day
Because of the late Martin Luther King Junior's birthday

BOUNCY, BUBBLY AND BEAUTIFUL

Bouncy, bubbly and beautiful is what you are to me
You have such a great and awesome personality
You are always so friendly to everyone you see
I'm sure that everyone around you feels the same way too
Bouncy, bubbly and beautiful is a great name for you

ORANGE NET SWEATER

She had on a beautiful orange net sweater
And she has pretty long hair too
She's a cutie pie, yes this is true
When she walks her hair swings back and forth
She looks like a beauty queen that's for sure
Orange net sweater, keep on looking beautiful like you do
And always remember that Jesus loves you

HAZEL EYES AND A BEAUTIFUL SWEATER

Wow I saw a beautiful lady just the other day
She had the most beautiful hazel eyes that I have ever seen
She had on a beautiful sweater
And a bling bling bracelet too
I thought, you go girl
You are really looking good
She said it was from her daughter
A special gift for her
She will always remember this poem I made for her

SWEET FRAGRANCE

One day a sweet fragrance filled the air
I had to look around to see from where
I turned around to see a beautiful lady walk past me
I said, is that you that smells so good
And she said, yes that's me
Then she smiled and went on her way
I think I made her happy the rest of the day

BEAUTY QUEEN

I saw a little girl next to me she is very pretty yes indeed
She has beautiful curly hair and two pink bows
And she has a little cute tutu on
She looks like she could be in a picture show
Her mom told her to say hi
She smiled and waved at me
Oh she looked like a little beauty queen
Oh how she inspired me
That is why she is in my book you see
Beauty queen, keep on looking beautiful like you do
And always remember that Jesus loves you

HANDSOME AND BEAUTIFUL

Handsome and beautiful you both are to me
You are both so precious, precious as can be
You have a great personality this is what I see
I will miss seeing you and your handsome baby too
Keep your focus in everything that you do
Your little handsome baby really needs you
And you need him too
I pray the best for you
And always remember that Jesus loves you

RING AND MATCHING BLOUSE

Your ring and your matching blouse is beautiful too
Everything you wear looks so pretty on you
You're an amazing young lady
And you're very beautiful too
God really blessed us by sending us you

PENCILS AND PENS IN HER HAIR

I met a lady who always has pencils and pens in her hair
If she needs to write a note she is always prepared
She has an earring in her lip and one in her nose
She is a pretty, pretty lady yes everybody knows
She is very, very kind whenever she speaks to me
And she always treats me so very respectfully
Pencils and pens, I appreciate you
And always remember that Jesus loves you

PINK AND BLACK SHOES

I saw a beautiful lady the other day
I noticed her pink and black shoes right away
She also had on a pink hoodie too
I thought, wow it really looks good on you
Her face lit up light a Christmas tree
I believe she enjoyed the compliment
That she received from me
Pink and black, keep on looking cute like you do
And always remember that Jesus loves you

PRETTY LADY, PRETTY CURLY HAIR

I met a pretty lady with pretty curly hair
She came to get her friend some ice while she was sick upstairs
She had a smile upon her face, a very joyful glow
She said her son had a basketball game and she was ready to go
Later I saw her again and she was with her son
I could tell by the look on her face that her son's team had won
So anyway I asked them if his team had won the game
They were both so excited, YES they did proclaim!

BEAUTIFUL FAMILY PICTURE

A lady showed me her beautiful family picture the other day
Wow her picture was really beautiful I must say
They were all dressed in beautiful array
Red and white was their color that day
They were all filled with Christmas cheer
Oh how the lady was filled with joy
To have her beautiful daughters and her handsome boy
Soon they would open up their gifts
And enjoy each other's company
That was her greatest gift

A BEAUTIFUL OWL TATOO

The other day I saw a lady with a beautiful owl tattoo
The amazing thing about it, it wasn't brown, but a colorful blue
I looked at her face and she was also beautiful too
Her makeup really brought out the color of her beautiful owl tattoo
She is blessed with children and one on the way too
And I'm sure they also love looking at her beautiful owl tattoo
The other day she had on a jacket of many colors
I was reminded of a Bible story of Joseph and his brothers
Joseph also had a coat of many colors

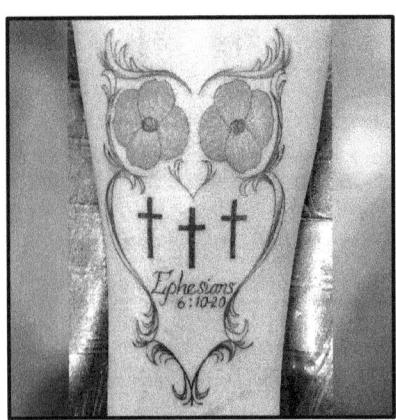

CURLY HAIR AND FRENCH BRAIDS

I saw a girl with curly hair
At the ice machine
I said, wow your hair is beautiful
And she turned and smiled at me
And then she said, thank you very cheerfully

Then I saw her another day
With French braids in her hair
Then I told her, wow you still look good
No matter what style you wear

GENEROUS GIVER

Generous giver is what you are to me
It is the love of God that's in you I see
You are always quick to give a helping hand
You are a one of a kind special friend
When you give it comes back to you
I pray that God's blessings constantly come back to you
I love you and appreciate you
And always remember that Jesus loves you

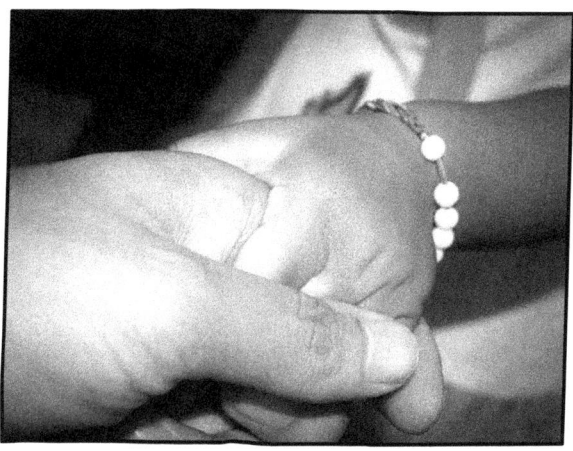

EXCITED

You were so excited to get a poem
And I was so excited to write one for you too
You have the most beautiful brown eyes
And you have a very pretty smile too
Your white jacket diamond ring
And your beautiful bracelet really looks good on you
You make me smile and I hope I make you smile too
God bless you, I pray the best for you
You, were excited to get a poem
And I was excited to write one for you

HANDSOME YOUNG MAN

You are a very handsome young man
And you are very respectful too
You love your mom very much
And she also loves you too
You do such a good job honoring your mom
That's what the Bible says to do
Any mom would be glad to have a wonderful son like you
You love Jesus, and Jesus loves you too

BRIGHT COLORS

You are so beautiful
And your bright colors are beautiful too
I really like your colored sweater
And your bright colored hoodie too
But most of all I like the beautiful smile that I receive from you
Stay focused on your recovery no matter what you do
You made it this far, you can make it all the way through

BLUE AND RED

One day you had on a pretty red sweater
The next day I saw you with a blue jacket and cute boots
I thought, wow she looks amazing
I like looking at the new you
Also I want to tell you thank you
For always saying thank you for your food
I will always remember the kind words that I receive from you
You're a beautiful young lady
And always remember that Jesus loves you too

I FELT GOD'S LOVE

Two little boys gave me a hug
And they told me that they loved me too
My heart leaped for joy
That was such a kind thing for them to do
This is a great memory that I will think on all of my life
God reminded me that He loved me not once but twice
I felt God's love, keep on sharing love like you do
And always remember that Jesus loves you

WONDERFUL TEAM PLAYER & AWESOME COOK

You're a wonderful team player
And you're an awesome cook too
I really enjoy your food
And I love working with you too
We work really well together
And I crave your yummy food
I love you very much
And Jesus loves you too

CUTE SWEATER AND PRETTY GREEN EYES

I love your cute sweater and your pretty green eyes too
But most importantly I love the kindness I receive from you
You love your boys very much
And they also love you too
And by the way, they are all very handsome
I can see that they get their good looks from you
I love your cute sweater and your pretty green eyes too

I HOPE TO SEE YOU FOR A LONG TIME

I hope to see you for a long time and your wonderful son too
My days seems so much brighter every time I see both of you
Your smile and kind spirit inspired me to write this poem for you
You are an amazing young lady and you are very beautiful too
And always remember that Jesus loves you

YOU LOOK LIKE A MODEL TO ME

You look like a model to me
From your hair down to your feet
I love your curly hair and your makeup too
It really brings out the beauty in you
You look like a model to me
And I really love your great personality
Stay focused on your dreams they can come true
How hard you work at them is all up to you
And always remember that Jesus loves you

FIFTY PURSES, WIGS, AND SHOES

She has 50 purses, wigs, and shoes
And she is really beautiful too
Whatever she wants to wear
She matches I declare
She also has a cute shape
Which makes everything stay in place
Fifty purses, wigs, and shoes, keep on looking cute like you do
And always remember that Jesus loves you

ALWAYS KIND TO US

For the 3½ years that we have known you
You have always been kind to us
We appreciate the smile on your face
And the respect that you always have for us
We pray the best for you
And your wonderful children too
Always share your testimony
Of how God has helped you make it through
It will make you strong and help others too
We love you and Jesus loves you too

BROWN EYES AND GLOWING FACE

*I love your beautiful brown eyes
And your beautiful glowing face too
Your glowing face is one of the first things I noticed
The day I first saw you
Your daughter is also very special
And she has beautiful brown eyes just like you
You're a very special young lady
And always remember that Jesus Christ loves you*

SHE ALWAYS REMEMBERS OUR NAMES

*She is a beautiful lady I have known for a while
And she is very special too
She always remembers our names
And she says them with a smile too
Thank you for always remembering our names
And thank you for always being respectful too
And always remember that Jesus loves you*

AMAZING YOUNG LADY

*You are an amazing young lady
And you are very beautiful too
Your daughters are also beautiful
And they are sweet and kind just like you
Your son is also very handsome
And he is very special too
I appreciate your smile and your great attitude
You're an amazing young lady
And you are very beautiful too
And always remember that Jesus loves you*

SPECIAL BOY

You're a very special boy
And you're very handsome too
I love your pretty blonde hair
And your great personality too
Thank you for getting your mom's food
She loves you very much
And she is so very proud of you
Your mom does a lot for you
Its okay to help her too
You're a very special boy
And you are very handsome too

BROWN EYES AND LIGHT-UP SHOES

You're a beautiful girl
And your brown eyes are beautiful too
I really like your light up shoes
They really look pretty on you
You love being with your mommy
And she loves being with you too
You both are very special
And always remember that Jesus loves you too

LONG HAIR, SMILE & FRENCH BRAIDS

I love your long hair, your smile, and your French braids too
But most importantly I love your wonderful attitude
Stay focused in all that you do
And always keep your wonderful attitude
You can do whatever you set your mind to do
And always remember that Jesus loves you

THE MAN WHO SMILES EVERY DAY

Whenever I walk by him he always has a smile for me
He is very special, special yes indeed
He is also handsome I'm sure that everyone agrees
He is a very hard worker there is not a lazy bone in him
He also loves his son and he is handsome just like him
Keep on smiling every day, I really appreciate you
And always remember that Jesus loves you too

EYELASHES, SMILE & CURLY HAIR

You're a beautiful lady I declare
I love your eyelashes, your smile and your curly hair
Your boy is handsome and you're beautiful
I can see he gets his good looks from you
You are doing a good job with your son
Stay focused on all that you do
You need your son and he needs you too
You're a very special young lady
And always remember that Jesus loves you

BLACK AND WHITE JUMPSUIT

I really love your black and white jumpsuit
And I love your curly hair too
You are one beautiful lady
And I appreciate the kindness I receive from you
You can make it through the program
Just stay focused on what you need to do
And always remember that Jesus loves you

WHITE JEANS AND COLORFUL TENNIS SHOES

You are so beautiful
And you're a kind young lady too
You look real cute in your white jeans
And your colorful tennis shoes
Thank you for always saying hi to me
And thank you for always having such a good attitude
I always enjoy seeing you when I'm at work
And I will always remember you
Your smile is always encouraging to me
Jesus loves you and Jesus loves me

STAR OF THE SHOW

I went to watch the children sing
On a beautiful sunny day
As I looked forward I saw a beautiful girl singing every word
With a big smile upon her face
Oh how she was having so much fun
As she sang with her class that day

Then it was time to dance
And she really started to party
Star of the show, you were amazing
And you're very beautiful too
Keep on using your beautiful singing voice
And always remember that Jesus loves you

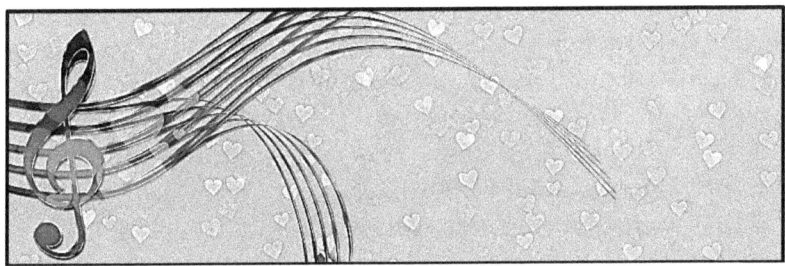

CUTE BOOT HOUSE SHOES AND RED HAIR

I really like your red hair,
And your cute boot house shoes too
Your house shoes look very comfortable
And I'm sure that your feet appreciate them too
I love your beautiful smile
And your great personality too
You can make it through the program
Stay focused on what you need to do
You're a beautiful young lady
And always remember that Jesus loves you

CLEANING MACHINE AND WHIRLWIND

There are two amazing ladies who I see just about every day
Cleaning Machine and Whirlwind yes that is their names
They work so fast and clean, clean, clean, all throughout the day
I appreciate their hard work and the kindness they portray
You are two amazing young ladies
And you are very pretty too
Keep up the good job
And always remember that Jesus loves you

GRAY ZIPPER BOOTS, SMILE & CURLY HAIR

Your smile and your curly hair
Are two of the first things that I noticed about you
And I love your gray zipper boots, oh they are so cool
But you know you look good in anything that you wear
You look like a model I declare
You go girl, keep on doing what you do
And always remember that Jesus loves you

BLING JACKET & BEAUTIFUL NECKLACES

I love your bling jacket and your beautiful necklaces too
And I also love your beautiful smile and your great attitude
You are always thankful and never complain to me
You are one that my heart rejoices to see
Thanks for the kindness that I always receive from you
And always remember that Jesus loves you

PRETTY KITCHEN HELPER

There was a lady who worked with us a little while ago
She was very pretty don't you know
She loved working in the kitchen
And she did a really good job washing dishes
She also did whatever we needed her to do
She never complained because she has a great attitude
Her daughter is pretty like her
Both of them I really adore
Thank you for all that you do
And always remember that Jesus loves you

YOUR MOTHER'S LOVE

Wow I see the message loud and clear
Your mother loves you, my dear
She bought you pillowcases to embrace
So that the words of love would always be in your face
As you lay down at night and sleep
The words I love you
Will forever be in your memory
And then as you look at the pillowslip with the heart
Her love will keep you from falling apart

ONE-YEAR-OLD

He's a one-year-old and he is really cool
And his curly hair is very beautiful too
He has a smile that lights up the room
Whenever he sees me he smiles at me and I smile at him too

I love talking to him when he is in his class
Sometimes he looks at me and gives me a little laugh
He gets his good looks from his mom
He has her heart and she loves him so much
She loves to hug him with her tender touch
One-year-old, you are cool and very special too
And always remember that Jesus loves you

PURPLE COLORADO HOODIE

I met a new lady a few days ago
She is very beautiful don't you know
She had on a purple Colorado hoodie
And a beautiful smile on her face
She is one of the prettiest ladies in this place

At first she was so shy when we first met
Now she's warming up to me
And our conversation is getting better yet
Purple Colorado hoodie
I hope that this poem encourages you
And always remember that Jesus loves you

LONG TIME COWORKER FRIEND

There's a beautiful lady I've known for many years
She worked with the teens and their children
And cared for them like they were her own kids
Whenever I see her I always have good thoughts
She has a heart to help people who are hurting
In any way that she can
I appreciate her and consider her my friend
I hadn't seen her for a while
But today I saw her again
I was so glad to see my long time coworker friend
Coworker friend, keep on doing the good job that you do
And always remember that Jesus loves you

GRAPE SHAMPOO

I was in the window the other day
When a good smell came my way
I thought, wow that Kool-Aid really smells good
Then I turned around and to my surprise
There was a beautiful lady standing in front of my eyes
Then I said, is that smell coming from you
She said, yes it's my grape shampoo
I told her, wow you really smell good
Then she smiled and went on her way
I think I made her happy that day
I appreciate the good smell that came from you
And always remember that Jesus loves you

CLEAN RAP

I met a boy a while ago
He is very handsome don't you know
He also loves to do a rap
He is very good as a matter of fact
I also love his curly hair
And his smile is amazing I declare
Sometimes he likes to give me a hug
Or he pushes a cart
He is such a sweetheart
Clean rap, you're really cool
And always remember that Jesus loves you

BLACK RUFFLE SWEATER AND SHOES

I saw a beautiful lady the other day
She had on two amazing things
A black ruffle sweater with matching shoes
I told her, you look amazing, you really do
If I was a photographer I would love to take her pictures
And put them on display
Because she looks so beautiful every single day
Black ruffled sweater and shoes, keep looking beautiful like you do
And always remember that Jesus loves you

BLUE AND SILVER JACKET

I like your blue and silver jacket and your colorful pants too
I also love your beautiful smile and your curly hair too
You are sweet just like your mom and you both are beautiful too
Your mom is blessed to have a beautiful daughter like you
And always remember that Jesus loves you

SWEET AND KIND

Sweet and kind that's what you are to me
Whenever I see you, you always have a smile for me
You're one sweet lady, I really adore you
And I'm sure that all of your friends adore you too
God has given you a great personality
This is one thing that I noticed about you
Stay sweet and kind no matter where you go or what you do
I hope that this poem brings encouragement to you
And always remember that Jesus loves you

BLUE EYES AND CUTE HAIRSTYLE

I saw a beautiful lady the other day
She had beautiful blue eyes and a cute hairstyle, hey, hey, hey
When she walked, her hair stayed in place
And the style that she had really complemented her face
I told her that her hair looked cute that day
She smiled and said, thank you, and went on her way

RED PLAID SHIRT AND BLUE EYES

I like your red plaid shirt and your blue eyes too
But most of all I like the warm personality
That God has given to you
You are a beautiful young lady and you're a great babysitter too
I'm sure the mothers and children feel the same way about you
Thanks for always smiling and treating me so respectfully
I appreciate you
And always remember that Jesus loves you

LOVE FOR CHILDREN

You have a love for children
And they have a love for you too
I believe that God has given
A special heart to you
You love to play with them and hug them too
You're like a big sister to them
I'm sure that is what they think about you
I love your beautiful long hair
And your great personality too
You're a beautiful young lady
And always remember that Jesus loves you

THIRTY-ONE YEARS WORKING WITH CHILDREN

Congrats beautiful lady
I am so proud of you
Thirty-one years working with children
Not many could do what you do
You love the children with all of your heart
It shows in everything that you do
If I was a kid I would be glad
To have a great teacher like you
You talk to the children on their level
And you also enjoy singing to them too
Thirty-one years working with children
Keep up the good job that you do
And always remember that Jesus loves you

BABOCHE

Baboche, Baboche, Baboche, Baboche

I'm a grandma rapper and my purpose in life
Is to deny myself and give my life to Christ
When I wake up in the morning and it's time to pray
I get down on my knees and say
Jesus, you're the one for me
Jesus, you died to set me free

Baboche, Baboche, Baboche, Baboche

All you girls at House of Mercy
This is a transitional facility
You're here to get your life on track
You're here to get your children back
Baboche

BONNET BABY

I saw a little baby one day
She was very beautiful I must say
She had a little bonnet on her head
She made me smile again and again
Then another day when I saw her
She had on a sleeper with bunny prints
And on her feet were little bunnies
Oh they were so cute and funny

Me, the baby, and her mommy laughed
We had fun on the elevator and that's a fact
I really enjoy her little baby
She always has a big smile for me
Bonnet baby, keep on looking cute like you do
And always remember that Jesus loves you

GRAY HAIR AND GREEN TENNIS SHOES

I met a lady the other day
She had pretty long gray hair and a beautiful face
I also liked her green tennis shoes
They were very bright and pretty cool
She said she earned every gray hair
I said I understood as she declared
I appreciate how you are always kind to me
And also how you always have a smile for me
You are so precious, and your friend is precious too
And always remember that Jesus loves you

PINK SWEATER NECLACE & EARRINGS

You always look so pretty
But today you look extra cute
I love your pink sweater necklace
And your earrings too
You should wear pink more often
It really brings out the beauty in you
When I see you all dressed up
You make me want to dress up too

MOTHER'S KISS

You love your baby and your baby loves you too
As you kiss him on his cheek he feels lots of love from you
You're a beautiful young lady
And your yellow hat is very beautiful too
Mother's kiss, keep on loving your baby like you do
And always remember that Jesus loves you

BLOUSE FROM HER MOTHER

I met a new lady today
She is very pretty I must say
I loved her cute curly hairdo
And her beautiful smile too
She had on a beautiful blouse from her mother
Her blouse was so pretty
I could stare at it all day long
Until I see you again, thanks for all that you do
And always remember that Jesus loves you

STREAKED HAIR AND PRETTY SCARF

I met a new lady today
She was very beautiful I must say
She had the most beautiful streaked colored hair
And very pretty scarf around her neck I declare
Even though it's my first time meeting you,
I look forward to getting to know you
I appreciate all that you do
And always remember that Jesus loves you

HANDSOME HELPER

There is a boy who likes to talk to me
And whenever he gets a chance
He likes to help push a cart for me
He loves sports and he is really cool
He is also a good helper for his mother too
Handsome helper, keep on doing the good job that you do
And always remember that Jesus loves you

PRECIOUS BABY

Precious, precious, he's so precious to me
Wrapped in his blue, white, and gray little blankie
His mom's face lit up with joy
Because she finally had her precious baby boy
Precious baby, you're a gift from heaven above
God blessed your mommy with you to show her His love

PURPLE AND BLACK BLOUSE

Wow, look at you today
I really like your beautiful purple and black blouse, hey, hey, hey
You are so amazing to me
And you always dress so very pretty
Wow grape smelling hair and a cute face
You are one of the prettiest girls in this place
And I always enjoy seeing your face
Purple and black blouse, I appreciate you
And always remember that Jesus loves you

CURLY HAIR AND ROSE SWEATER

I saw a girl in the dining room
She had on a beautiful black blouse with rose designs
And oh her hair was looking so fine
Her mom did her hair a special way
She really liked it I could tell by the smile on her face
When I see her she's always so kind to me
And she always has a big smile for me
Curly hair and rose sweater, your mom loves you
And always remember that Jesus loves you too

BLACK LACE BLOUSE & HIGH HEEL BOOTS

As I walked down the hallway the other day
A beautiful lady walked past me
Wow she was looking so very, very, pretty
She had on a beautiful black lace blouse and high heel boots
She walked with confidence
She knew she was looking cute
So I went to tell her, wow you are looking good
She said, thank you, and smiled
Like I knew she would

FANCY BLOUSE WITH A CROSS

I met a beautiful lady today
With blonde hair and pink streaks
She also had a fancy blouse with a cross
Decorated with bling bling
She look so cute she made me want to sing
She had bling bling on her shoulders too
I thought, you go girl look at you
Keep on looking cute like you do
And always remember that Jesus loves you

ABC SHIRT AND ZEBRA PANTS

I saw a little baby the other day
She had on an ABC shirt and zebra pants
She looked so cute and that's a fact
I talked to her and tickled her tummy
She got so excited she laughed and laughed

ABOVE AND BEYOND

She stopped to help me when things were a mess
She could tell that I was a little bit stressed
I was in a hurry to get done
Then I was bombarded all at once
She said, don't worry I'll take care of it for you
I know that you have other things you need to do
So she cleaned up the water mess that someone else made
She was a big help
She made my day
Above and beyond, thanks for all that you do
And always remember that Jesus loves you

ENCOURAGING LADY

You're a very beautiful lady
And you are very precious too
I appreciate the kindness
I always receive from you
So many times when I have been down
And full of doubt instead of faith
Your messages have given me strength
To make it another day
So thank you, encouraging lady
I love you and I appreciate you too
But most importantly
Always remember that Jesus loves you too

FACE LIKE AN ANGEL

When I looked at your baby
Oh she was so precious to me
She had a face like an angel
This is one thing I did see
Her skin was so soft, soft yes indeed
While her eyes were closed
I saw a little smile on her face
She was dreaming happy dreams
Because she felt her mommy's love and embrace

HOPEFUL AGAIN

I watched you when you first came
You seemed to be really down
When your son came to be with you again
I saw your frown turn into a smile
Oh how my heart rejoiced with you
When you heard the good news

Your self-esteem was lifted
You said goodbye to all the blues
Now keep your head up
Don't let anyone or anything get you down
Your son loves you very much
And he needs you to stick around
I believe that God spoke these words from me to you
And always remember that Jesus loves you

SPECIAL CARD

My boss received a special card from her friend
Because she has been with her through thick and thin
When she was up and when she was down
She always seemed to be around
She also sent her a heart necklace on Valentine's Day
It's a heart connection that they have with each other
They are like sisters even though they have different mothers
It is very rare to have some good friends
So when you get some you hold to them
Special card, you are one of a kind
I also consider you a friend of mine
Keep on loving people like you do
And always remember that Jesus loves you

HE LOVES BASKETBALL

I met a boy the other day
He really liked basketball I must say
He was dribbling the ball in the dining room
Then he went up for a hoop like he was making a real shot
He was so happy he was dropping it like it was hot
He loves his mom a lot and she thinks he's pretty cool
On top of all of that he is really handsome too
He loves basketball, I really like you
And always remember that Jesus loves you

MOMMA'S HEARTBEAT

Momma's heartbeat is what I see when I look at you
It's amazing the love that generates from her to you
Her heart gets so excited whenever she's around you
You're her special boy and she loves you
l love seeing you hug him and hold him in your arms
I can see that you have a very special bond
He is one handsome boy this is true
I can see he gets his good looks from you
Momma's heartbeat
You're blessed to have a wonderful mother like you do
And always remember that Jesus loves you

HEART TATTOO AND BEAUTIFUL NICKNAME

Your heart tattoo is beautiful
And your nickname is beautiful too
Your heart tattoo is one of the first things I remember
The day I first met you
You also have a fun personality and a beautiful smile too
You always seem to be so thankful every time I see you
Stay focused on your recovery, great things await you
And always remember that Jesus Christ loves you

KOBE TENNIS SHOES & ORANGE SOCKS

I saw a guy by the elevator the other day
He was very handsome I must say
Then I happened to look down and what did I see?
Orange socks and Kobe tennis shoes, they were so cool to me
I said, wow I really like your orange socks
And your Kobe tennis shoes
Then he smiled and said, thank you
Then he went to do whatever he had to do
Kobe tennis shoes, keep on looking cool like you do
And always remember that Jesus loves you

BOOK AND HEADPHONES

I saw a beautiful lady yesterday
She was having a good time I must say
She was sitting at the table reading a book with her head phones on
Oh how she was dancing, dancing in her seat
I'm sure she was listening to a groovy beat
She really made me laugh that day
To see her having fun that way
Book and headphones, keep on having fun like you do
And always remember that Jesus Christ loves you

GREEN-EYED TWINS

I saw two little babies with beautiful green eyes
They were both so precious
I wanted to hold them on each one of my sides
One had on a cute hoodie and one had on a cute sweater
Their mom dressed them warm
Because that day it was chilly weather

BUTTERFLY BLOUSE

I saw a lady the other day
She was very beautiful I must say
She had on a beautiful blouse with cute butterflies
And a pretty jacket that really caught my eyes
She always takes time to talk to me
And she always has a great smile for me
Butterfly blouse, keep on looking cute like you do
And always remember that Jesus loves you

DOLL FACE

I saw a beautiful little girl the other day
The amazing thing about her was her doll looking face
Wow she was as cute as they come
She had on a pink and green outfit from her grandma
Hearted butterflies and a pink rose in the corner of her top
You could tell that her grandma had fun when she shopped
Wow, mommy's little doll face
You can see she's a special part of your world
Doll face, keep on looking cute like you do
And always remember that Jesus loves you

FLOWER PANTS AND HEART SHIRT

I saw a little baby today
She was very beautiful I must say
She had the cutest little flowered pants on
And a heart shirt with bows on her upper arms
And a little cute tutu which really topped it all off
Flower pants and heart shirt, keep on looking cute like you do
And always remember that Jesus loves you

BLUE FLOWERED DRESS

I met a lady the other day
She is very beautiful I must say
She is pregnant, yes indeed
She is getting ready to have her special little baby
She had on a very beautiful flowered dress
She looked so happy and so blessed
Blue flowered dress, I think you're special, yes I do
I look forward to getting to know you
And always remember that Jesus loves you

KITTY CAT SHIRT

I saw a pretty little girl outside one day
She had a very amazing T-shirt on I must say
She had a picture of my favorite pet
A beautiful kitty cat
And when I looked a little closer to my surprise
The kitty cat had flowers on her head that really caught my eyes
Kitty cat T-shirt, keep on looking beautiful like you do
And always remember that Jesus loves you

HE LOVES TO SING THE OLDIES

A lady told me, this is something you can write about
My son he loves to sing oldies and he has a lot of favorite ones
She said he knows the words and he can sing too
I'm sure that when he reads this he will feel very special
Because of the kind words spoken about him from you
He loves to sing oldies, keep on having fun singing like you do
And by the way you are very handsome too
And always remember that Jesus loves you

ORCHARD FLOWER

*When I was trying to think of something to write about you
You're like a flower came to my mind
So I asked your mom what beautiful flower reminded her of you
And orchard came to her mind so this is what I wrote about you
An orchard is beautiful inside and out and so are you
And also your kindness is like a sweet orchard
And a beautiful fragrance comes from you
Your mom seems extremely happy whenever she's with you
Your mom loves you very much
And Jesus loves you too*

HE LOVES CATS

*When I asked a lady to tell me something special about her son
She said he loves cats, well I love cats too
So to me her answer was really cool
She said he loves to meow and act like a cat
Well sometimes I do too, so I laughed about that
He loves cats, keep on loving our favorite animal like you do
And always remember that Jesus loves you*

TWO-TONED COLORED HAIR

*I met a lady the other day
She was very beautiful I must say
She had some of the most beautiful two-toned colored hair
She looked really pretty I declare
Then I looked at her neck she had on a rainbow string for her keys
And some diamond earrings with a lot of bling
You go girl, keep on looking cute like you do
And always remember that Jesus loves you*

FLOWING HAIR

I saw a lady a few days ago
She was very pretty don't you know
She had some of the most beautiful blonde flowing hair
When she walked away from the window
Her hair bounced and flowed
And oh her good smelling perfume
Quickly came up to my nose
As I sniffed the air my nose was so happy I declare
I wanted to follow her everywhere
Flowing hair, keep on looking pretty
And smelling good like you do
And always remember that Jesus loves you

CROSS AND ORANGE LAYERD BLOUSE

There is a lady I have worked with for a while
She has a great personality and a beautiful smile
She loves talking to the woman and children
And rocking the babies too
She really cares a lot about people
It shows in everything that she does
I'm sure that it's because of her heavenly Father
Who has filled her with so much love

She has a cross tattooed on the back of her neck,
She loves Jesus, she loves to represent
The other day she had on a beautiful orange layered blouse
And she also showed her big pretty smile
Cross and orange layered blouse, keep on loving people like you do
And always remember that Jesus loves you

PATCH QUILT

I saw a beautiful lady today
She had a new baby, hey, hey, hey
He was wrapped in his cute quilt
Snuggled in his mother's arms
He felt safe and secure
He knew that she would keep him from harm
He smiled then he went to sleep
Being safe in his mother's arms gave him great relief
Patch quilt, you're one of a kind
And you are always on your mommy's mind
You're a very handsome baby this is true
And always remember that Jesus loves you

SWEETER THAN COTTON CANDY

Sweeter than cotton candy is what comes to my mind
When I think about you
Because your kindness is so genuine
Whenever I see you
You're always so thankful
You never gripe or complain
I'm sure everyone that hangs around you
Feels the same way

Don't be discouraged
You're a blessing to me
And also to your wonderful baby
Sweeter than cotton candy
Keep on doing what you do
And always remember that Jesus loves you

SALAD LADY

There's a beautiful lady I see almost every night
She always has a smile and she is always so nice
She always comes to get a plate
Salad first, she always says
Then she comes back to get her main course plate
She's always early, never late
This world would be a better place
If there were more people like you
Keep on eating your salad that's good for you
And always remember that Jesus loves you

DADDY'S LITTLE GIRL BLOUSE

I saw a little girl the other day
She had on a Daddy's little girl blouse
And a big smile upon her face
Then I looked down at her feet
And she had on converse tennis shoes
I thought, you go girl
You are really looking cute
Then she smiled at me
And her and her mom went away
She was very proud to wear
Daddy's little girl blouse that day
Daddy's little girl blouse, keep on looking cute like you do
And always remember that Jesus loves you

CUTE OFFICE

I went into my coworker's office a while ago
It was very cute don't you know
She had black, pink, and white tissue paper flowers
On her polka dot board on her wall,
And beautiful flowers in her windowsill
I remember them most of all
Her office was so cozy
I could have just sat with her and talked
But it was time for me to go so I said goodbye
It's time for me to get on the clock

KIDS GIVE YOU HOPE

I saw a pretty lady one day
We were passing each other in the hallway
I said hi and asked her how she was doing
She said she had a visit with her kids
Because of them she had hope to get up out of bed
Oh how that inspired me so to hear that she had hope
I finally got to meet her kids
They are precious yes indeed
I can see why they make her a happy mommy
Kids give you hope, keep on being inspired by your kids like you do
Even though there are some challenging times too
I pray the best for you
And always remember that Jesus loves you

MICKEY MOUSE FOOTIE PAJAMAS

I saw a little boy the other day
He was very handsome I must say
He had on Mickey Mouse footie pajamas
He was on his way to snack
And he had the most beautiful blue eyes
As a matter of fact

His mom was also beautiful too
I thought, wow he gets his good looks from you
Mickey Mouse Footie Pajamas
Keep on looking handsome like you do
And always remember that Jesus loves you

BRAVE HEART

I met a boy in the dining room one day
He was very handsome I must say
He finally came to be with his mom
When I asked her to tell me something special about him
She said that he was brave
Because he helped take care of his younger siblings

Brave Heart, that name really fits you
There are not many who are as brave as you
Congrats on a job well done
Your mom loves you and cares about you too
That is why she hugs and kisses you
Brave Heart, I look forward to getting to know you
And always remember that Jesus loves you

TUTU TOP AND MATCHING SKIRT

I saw a little girl in the dining room one day,
She had on a tutu skirt and a matching top
She had a big smile on her face
Because her mommy dressed her really cute always
Then I looked at her hair
It also looked very cute I declare
Tutu top and matching skirt
You're blessed to have a mommy who cares about you
And always remember that Jesus loves you

BLING BLING HEADBAND AND SHOES

I was in the window today
When I looked up who did I see?
A beautiful baby girl
And her mom standing in front of me
As usual she was all dressed up just for me to see
She had bling bling on her headband
And sparkly bling tennis shoes too
I thought, you look like a fashion model, yes you do
She had a smile as if to say, yes my mommy loves me
And she always dresses me up so pretty
Bling, bling, headband and shoes, keep on looking cute like you do
And always remember that Jesus loves you

ZIGZAG ZIPPER SHIRT

I was in the dining room when a beautiful lady walked past me
She had on a very unique shirt
It had zippers but they were in a zig zag
I thought, this shirt is really cool
I would like to have one too
I told her I liked her shirt
She smiled and went on her way
I think I made her happy that day
Zig zag zipper shirt, keep on looking cute like you do
And enjoy the poems that I made for you
And always remember that Jesus loves you

MIRROR SANDALS

When I was on the teen floor the other day
I saw a beautiful young lady standing next to me
Her hair was up in a bun all in place
And she had a pretty smile upon her face
Then I just happened to look down
Because something shiny caught my eyes
It was the reflection of her mirror sandals, what a surprise
I told her, I really like your sandals
Mirror sandals is what I will call you
She also had some fuzzy pink shorts on too
Yes, she was looking pretty cute
Mirror sandals, keep on looking cute like you do
And always remember that Jesus loves you

GOLDEN BROWN EYES

I met a beautiful lady a while ago
She has the most beautiful golden colored brown eyes
Don't you know
She also has beautiful long curly hair
She is pretty as a picture I declare
Your daughter is also beautiful too
I can see that she get her good looks from you
Oh how I love your pink fuzzy robe
It looks so nice and cozy especially when it's cold
Golden brown eyes and pink fuzzy robe
Keep on looking beautiful like you do
And always remember that Jesus loves you

REDHEADED DOLL

There's a lady I see almost every day
She is very beautiful I must say
She reminds me of a cute redheaded doll
Whether her hair is up or whether it's down
She is still one of the cutest ladies in town
She also has a great personality
And she always dresses very pretty
I have known her for a while
She always says hello with a smile
Redheaded doll, keep on looking cute like you do
And always remember that Jesus loves you

BEAUTIFUL BLUE EYES

I met a lady with beautiful blue eyes
And she has a kind personality too
She has a very soft spoken voice
I enjoyed the conversation between us too
She loves to talk to people
And she loves to sing to children too

SHE'S A MOMMA'S DREAM COME TRUE

Oh she waited for that special day
She gets to see her baby on a regular basis now, hey, hey, hey
Wow she's Momma's dream come true
And on top of that she is very beautiful too
She has a beautiful stroller and a cute blankie too
Full of colorful teddy bears, oh it's so cute
Oh how I love to see your smiling face
I can see that having your baby really makes your day
My heart rejoices with you
And always remember that Jesus loves you

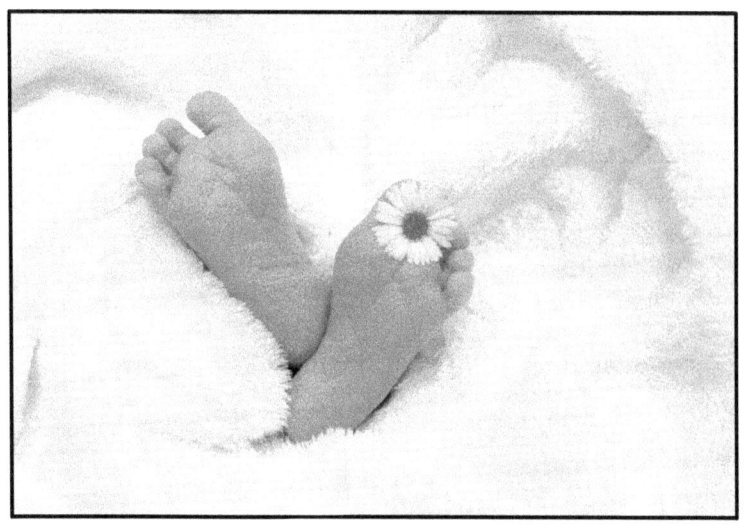

PLAID SHORTS

I saw a boy eating dinner one day
He had on cute plaid shorts and a very handsome face
He loves to be with his mom and she loves being with him too
They love each other very much yes they do
Plaid shorts, keep on loving your mom like you do
And always remember that Jesus loves you

SWEET LITTLE FACE

I met a new lady the other day
She had a beautiful smile and a cute little face
I told her that I wanted to make a poem for her
She was a beautiful lady that anyone would adore
I told her I wanted to put her in my book
She was so beautiful I had to take another look
Also she was very friendly
She's the kind of person you want to stay in your memory
Sweet little face, I really enjoyed meeting you
And always remember that Jesus loves you

MOMMA'S SPECIAL ROBE

I met a beautiful lady a little while ago
She was walking down the hallway
Wrapped up in her pretty pink robe
Come to find out her and her mother look a lot alike
She was wearing a special robe
That she got from her mom that night
Momma's special robe, keep on looking cute like you do
Your momma loves you very much
And Jesus loves you too

PRETTY GREEN AND BLING BLING

I saw a lady a while ago
She was really pretty don't you know
She had on a pretty green blouse
With bling bling on her neck
She always looks cute
She never looks a wreck
Pretty green and bling bling
Keep on looking cute like you do
And always remember that Jesus loves you

SPECIALIST LADIES

There are two beautiful ladies who I know
They are pretty cool, don't you know
They take time to talk to the parents and the children too
And when they have time they play with them too
They're beautiful and they're sweet
And they are also very kind to me
Specialist ladies, we all appreciate everything that you do
And always remember that Jesus loves you

BEAUTIFUL GREEN

I saw a young lady today
She was very beautiful I must say
She had on a green hoodie and green flip-flops
And green toenail polish which really topped it all off
I was so glad to see her all dressed in green
She looked very beautiful yes indeed
Beautiful green, keep on looking cute like you do
And always remember that Jesus loves you

WONDERFUL REDHEAD

I saw a new lady the other day
She was very beautiful I must say
She had a very beautiful smile
And her red hair was also cute
I really liked her style
Also her kids came to visit today
Beautiful and handsome could be their names
Wonderful redhead, keep on looking cute like you do
And always remember that Jesus loves you

HE'S A MAN WITH A VISION

He's a man with a vision which is plain to see
I have worked with him for twenty-two years
And he has always been an inspiration to me
He sets goals and sees them through
He does whatever he sets his mind to
He is tall and handsome and he always smells good too
His wife does a good job picking out his cologne
I give credit to her, and her alone
And oh he wears such nice suits and ties
He believes in looking good, that's no lie

Some think of him as a hard man, but in reality it's because
He has a lot of responsibility's in his hands
He cares about people who are hurting
And helps them in any way that he can
He strives to keep his vision alive
And he has many great team players on every side
So come aboard and catch the vision with him
He has already made up his mind that he is going to win
Man with a vision, thanks for all that you do
And always remember that Jesus loves you

BOPPING TO THE BEAT

I was in the window serving the other day
When I saw something that was cool I must say
A handsome little boy was in the arms of a beautiful young lady
She started bopping to the beat of her music
Then he started bopping too
I laughed and thought, wow he's mimicking you
They kept on bopping to the music as they went to find a seat
It was fun watching those two, they made me have a great evening
Bopping to the beat, keep on being cool
And always remember that Jesus loves you

HANDYMAN

There is a kind man who works at my job
And he is very gifted too
He fixed our air in the dishes room, salad and hot steamer shields
And also remodeled a wall in the kitchen
And made my boss' office look unique too
He's a handyman, he can do whatever he sets his mind to do
On top of all of that he is very handsome too
Handyman, thanks for the blessing you are to House of Mercy
We all appreciate you
And always remember that Jesus loves you

PINK FUR SWEATER

I saw a little girl today
She was very pretty I must say
She had on a beautiful pink sweater with ruffled lace
She looked like a little fashion model with a cute little face
She also had some of the prettiest hair
She was beautiful like her mom I declare
Pink fur sweater, keep on looking cute like you do
And always remember that Jesus loves you

THREE ROSES

I saw a beautiful lady by the elevator one day
She had 3 beautiful roses and a cute stuffed animal in her hands
I said, wow what's the special occasion, what's going on with you
She said it was her anniversary and she got roses from her man
I got so excited for her I almost clapped my hands
She said the roses represented the love he had for her
And the baby inside that they one day would share
It's so precious how he took the time to show her that he cared
Anyone would love to have that kind of man
Three roses, this was such a kind thing for you to do
And always remember that Jesus loves you

ONE OF A KIND HELPER

I saw a lady working hard the other day
She was doing such a good job I must say
She said that she was helping her friend while she was gone
I thought, wow she will be surprised when she gets home
I told my boss to look at the work that the lady did
She was also impressed as she smiled and nodded her head
I told her, I'm going to do something nice for you
There's an extra place in my book just for you
One of a kind helper, keep on doing a good job like you do
And always remember that Jesus loves you

BEAUTIFUL DESIGN AND A CROSS

I saw a lady today
She was very beautiful I must say
She had on black pants and a beautiful black and gray bracelet
That matched her blouse
Her designs were so amazing
I had to give her a big shout
Then I looked at her neck
And she had on a big cross
Which reminded me of Jesus
Wow that really topped it off
Beautiful designs and a cross
Keep on looking cute like you do
And always remember that Jesus loves you

CHANGING EYE COLOR

I met a lady the other day
She was very beautiful I must say
She had on a beautiful heart necklace and a rainbow ring
And one of the most beautiful blouses that I have ever seen
Also at any time her eyes can be blue, gray, or green
She is a real cutie pie yes indeed
You are beautiful inside and out
Don't let anyone make you doubt
Changing eye color, keep on looking cute like you do
And always remember that Jesus loves you

PURPLE LACE

I saw a little baby the other day
She was very beautiful I must say
She had on a beautiful tutu with built in leggings
And a purple and white tee-shirt with a big purple bow
She looked like she was going to a special dress up show
Purple lace, keep on looking cute like you do
And always remember that Jesus loves you

SPLATTER PAINT JACKET & JEANS

I saw a little girl the other day
She had on a splatter paint jacket with matching jeans
Oh she looked so cute and clean
I was so inspired when I saw her
I just had to write a poem for her
Her mom smiled because she was her little girl
And because she brought the cute outfit for her
Splatter paint jacket and jeans, keep on looking cute like you do
And always remember that Jesus loves you

BROKEN KEY OUT OF LOCK

When I told you the problem you came and helped me
You didn't even complain, you did it cheerfully
Wow you really make a difference in everything that you do
And you are always quick to help whoever needs you
You are one amazing man
You show me that together we stand
Thanks again for all that you do
And always remember that Jesus loves you

GREEN SKIRT AND PRETTY FACE

I saw a beautiful lady today
She had on a green skirt and she had a very pretty face
Her skirt was really pretty I declare
And it also had a little bit of a flare
She is also an amazing lady too
And I really love her great attitude
Green skirt and pretty face, keep on looking cute like you do
And always remember that Jesus loves you

SWEET AS HONEY

Sweet as honey you are to me
It must be the love of Jesus in you that touches me
I have always liked you right from the start
You have such a kind and caring heart
The light of Jesus shines through you
I'm sure that others can see it too
Sweet as honey, keep on doing what you do
And always remember that Jesus loves you

BLUE EYES, CURLY HAIR & ROSE SHOES

I saw a beautiful girl in the waiting room today
She had the most beautiful curly hair and amazing blue eyes
She was so happy, finally her mom was right by her side
Then I looked down at her feet
She had on some cute shoes with roses on them
And they were pretty neat
Blue eyes, curly hair and rose shoes
I'm so glad I finally got to meet you
And always remember that Jesus loves you

TANK TOP AND PRETTY SANDALS

I was in the serving room the other day
When a beautiful lady came my way
She had on a beautiful colored tank top and pretty pink sandals too
She looked so cute I could tell she was in a good mood
She had her hair straight and flowing down
She was definitely one of the prettiest ladies in town
Tank top and pretty sandals, keep on looking cute like you do
And always remember that Jesus loves you

SWEET VOICE

I saw a lady the other day
She was very beautiful I must say
But the thing I remember most about her
Was her beautiful smile and her sweet voice
Someone else stepped before her in line
She said it was not a problem and she moved aside
We laughed together, then she went to eat her food
She made my day because she was in such a good mood
Sweet voice, I appreciate you
And always remember that Jesus loves you

FULL OF SMILES

When I was in the dining room last week
I met a little boy, oh he was so sweet
His mommy told him to say hi
And his face lit up with a smile
I said, since I got a big smile from you
Full of smiles is what I'll name you
He smiled and I walked away
I think I made him happy that day
Full of smiles, keep on smiling like you do
And always remember that Jesus loves you

MOTHER OF FOUR

She is a beautiful lady with four beautiful children
Oh how I love to see her every day
She comes to the window with a beautiful smile
I appreciate the kindness she displays
She loves her children very much
And they love her too
I watch you with your children
There's a special bond between them and you
You're a very special young lady
And always remember that Jesus loves you

BANANA PUDDING DELIGHT

The girls were so excited at dinner time last week
My boss made a very yummy banana pudding delight treat
She put pudding on the bottom, cool whip and Oreos on the top
Then she surrounded it with cherries, that really topped it off
The ladies and the kids were so excited as they ate every bite
They were all so very thankful for your banana pudding delight
Banana pudding delight, keep on making yummy things like you do
And always remember that Jesus loves you

COCONUT OIL

I walked past a lady the other day
When the smell of what she had on came my way
She said it was coconut oil in her hair
It really smelled good I declare
I want my hair to smell like hers
So I'm going to have to get me some
Coconut oil, thanks for smelling good like you do
And always remember that Jesus loves you

BLACK SWEATSHIRT AND PRETTY SMILE

I really like your black sweatshirt and your pretty smile too
The stars on the arm of your sweatshirt are really cool
You're an amazing young lady
And you're very special too
Your son is also very handsome
I can see that he gets his good looks from you
Stay focused on your recovery, you can make it through
And always remember that Jesus loves you

BLING BLING PURSE AND CUTE HAIRDO

I saw a beautiful lady the other day
She had a bling bling purse and a cute hairdo
I thought, you go girl look at you
Her bling bling purse really caught my eye
I thought, I could have a purse like that, why can't I?
When she walked away I thought, wow I really like that purse
I wonder how much it's worth
Bling, bling, purse and cute hairdo, keep on looking cute like you do
And always remember that Jesus loves you

BLUE DRESS AND POLKA DOT JACKET

I love your blue dress and your polka dot jacket too
And whatever hairstyle you have always looks good on you
You are an amazing young lady, and you are very beautiful too
I appreciate the smile and kindness that I always receive from you
You're a great example of House of Mercy's love
And I'm sure that all of the patients love you too
Just know that you're making a difference
And always remember that Jesus loves you

MOMMY'S TWIN

You're a very handsome boy
And your mom is very beautiful too
It is like I see double whenever I look at you two
You are very kind and respectful
Your mom sure did a good job teaching you
Any mom would be glad to have a wonderful son like you
Mommy's twin, keep on doing the good job that you do
And always remember that Jesus loves you

BRACELET MAKER

I met a lady the other day
She had a great personality and a pretty face
Then I looked down at her hands
She had some yarn and a crochet hook in her hands
And on her wrist she wore a beautiful band
The lady next to her had one too
She said, I don't just make them for myself but for others too
Bracelet maker, keep on doing what you do
And always remember that Jesus loves you

COOL GUITAR SHIRT

I saw a little boy some time ago
He was very handsome don't you know
He had a cool guitar shirt on
I noticed it when he was walking with his mom
He was really happy that day
As he held his mom's hand and they walked away
Cool guitar shirt, keep on looking cool like you do
And always remember that Jesus loves you

MY FRIEND'S HELPER

My friend's helper is beautiful, and she is very special too
She loves to help my friend do whatever she wants her to do
She always helps her with a smile and a great attitude
She has a beautiful smile and beautiful long hair too
My friend's helper, you are beautiful
And always remember that Jesus loves you

PRETTY CROCHETER

I met a girl the other day
She was very beautiful I must say
Her mom was beautiful too
I thought, wow she gets her good looks from you
Then I saw a pretty band around her head
She made it herself, her mom said
She knows how to make many things
She watched someone then she began to do her thing
Pretty crocheter, keep on doing what you do
And always remember that Jesus loves you

PURPLE TANK TOP

I saw a beautiful lady the other day
She had on a purple tank top and black and purple hair
She looked very beautiful I declare
Then I turned around and looked at her eyes
They were so beautiful I didn't look once, but twice
Purple tank top, I pray that things work out for you
And always remember that Jesus loves you

SAMPLE LADY

A new lady came to work with us recently
She is very beautiful and also very friendly
I encourage her and she encourages me
Thanks for helping me cut the roast
And everything else that you do
Sample lady, you are very kind
And always remember that Jesus loves you

MATCHING HEADBANDS

Her baby is adorable
This I can see
She has matching headbands to all of her clothes
From her beautiful mommy
As her mommy held her
She looked into her eyes
As I watched, it touched my heart with joy
And I almost cried
Matching headbands, keep on looking adorable like you do
And always remember that Jesus loves you

YOUR WORDS ARE IN MY MEMORY

A little while ago you said some kind words to me
To this day and forever they will stay in my memory
You said that I encouraged you whenever you felt down
Your words really touched my heart that day
And my face lit up with a smile
I know sometimes you get discouraged
And you know we all do
But always be careful what comes out of your mouth
Because your words are a big part of you
I think that you're very special
And you have a great sense of humor too
And always remember that Jesus loves you

LACE GREEN BLOUSE

I saw a girl a few days ago
She was very beautiful don't you know
She had on a beautiful lace green blouse
And she also had a beautiful smile
At first she seemed kind of shy
But now many times she says hi
I love to hear her sweet little voice
I look forward to talking to her more and more
Lace green blouse, keep on looking cute like you do
And always remember that Jesus loves you

SPEECHLESS

You're an amazing young lady
And you're very beautiful too
Speechless is one of the words that come to my mind
Whenever I think about you
When I saw you the other day
For a minute I couldn't even speak
Your beauty is so evident for everyone to see
Your inner beauty reflects on the outside of you
Beautiful, beautiful, beautiful you
Speechless, keep on sharing your beauty like you do
And always remember that Jesus loves you

VERY RESPECTFUL

I appreciate how you are very respectful to me
You respect my relationship with God
And that means a lot to me
Your words are like butter
On a yummy piece of warm cornbread
They slide into my heart and forever stay there
I love your beautiful face and your great attitude
I would love to have a friend
Who is as kind and caring as you
Very respectful lady, keep on doing what you do
And always remember that Jesus loves you

FUN BABYSITTER

I met a lady a little while ago
She was very beautiful don't you know
She's a babysitter for many of the kids
The thing that I remember most
Is that she has a lot of fun with them
She takes them for fun rides in their strollers
And likes to play with them too

Mothers love to have her watch their kids
Because they love how she takes care of them
Yesterday I found out that she likes to sing
I thought, you go girl, do your thing
Fun babysitter, keep on being a blessing to the kids like you do
And always remember that Jesus loves you

SWEET SMILE

You have one of the sweetest smiles that I have ever seen
And oh you are so precious to me
You love your kids, yes you do
And they also love their mommy too
I have known you for over one year
Whenever I see you, your sweet smile still appears
You have been blessed with a sweet smiling face
And you are such a blessing in this place
Sweet smile, I appreciate you
And always remember that Jesus loves you

BLACK WAVY HAIR AND CUTE LEATHER BOOTS

I was working on my books before work the other day
Then I looked up to check the clock so I wouldn't be late
And to my surprise who did I see?
A beautiful lady right in front of me
She had long black wavy hair
And her leather boots were really cute I declare
She had a pretty red plaid shirt around her waist
I thought, this young lady is really beautiful
And she has really good taste
Black wavy hair and cute leather boots
Keep on looking cute like you do
And always remember that Jesus loves you

HANDSOME HUNK

I saw a young man in the window the other day
He was a handsome hunk I must say
His mom was standing next to him
And she was very beautiful too
He looked so handsome
He could be a male model in a magazine
And she definitely could be a beauty queen
Wow a beautiful mom and handsome son team
And they also dress so nice and clean
Handsome hunk, it was a blessing meeting you
I appreciate your great attitude
And always remember that Jesus loves you

MOMMY'S LITTLE LADY

I saw a young girl the other day
She was very beautiful I must say
Her hair was long and feathered back
She had on a beautiful blouse and skirt too
And to top it all off she had on her mother's cute black boots
She looked like she was going out to eat
Or to some kind of special kids retreat
Wow I must say she looked like a little lady that day
Mommy's little lady, keep on looking cute like you do
And always remember that Jesus loves you

HER BABY IS SO BEAUTIFUL

Her baby is so beautiful, beautiful yes indeed
She looks like a doll out of a magazine
She dresses her so pretty from her head to her toes
Mommy loves her baby, everybody knows

SPAGHETTI DRESS

I saw a lady the other day
She was very beautiful I must say
She had on a beautiful black and white spaghetti dress
She looked like she was going to a nice place to eat
Yes she looked blessed
She walked around with confidence in her face
She was one of the prettiest ladies in this place
Spaghetti dress, keep on looking beautiful like you do
And always remember that Jesus loves you

COLORFUL TUTU SWIMMING SUITS

*I was in the dining room last week
When I saw a little girl who looked so sweet
She had a colorful tutu swimming suit on
And her hair was curly and long
Her mom said that her baby sister
Had a matching swimming suit too
I thought, I'm sure that they both looked so cute
Colorful tutu swimming suits, keep on looking cute like you do
And always remember that Jesus loves you*

PINK HOODIE

*I saw a lady in the dining room the other day
She was very beautiful I must say
She had a pink hoodie with the word love
And some bling bling jeans
Yes she was looking pretty clean
I was so happy to meet her that day
She is one of the prettiest girls in this place
Pink hoodie, keep on looking cute like you do
And always remember that Jesus loves you*

BLUE ZIPPER BOOTS

*My boss looked really pretty today
She wore a pretty dress, blue zipper boots, and white net stockings
She looked like a model I would say
Blue zipper boots, keep on looking cute like you do
And always remember that Jesus loves you*

PINK SWEATER

I met a lady the other day
She is very beautiful I must say
She had on a pink sweater with lace and gold letters
With the word "love" oh how her sweater inspired me
Now she is in my poem book you see
Her beautiful sweater will forever be in my memory
Pink sweater, keep on looking beautiful like you do
And always remember that Jesus loves you

TRIPLE HEART EARRINGS

I met a beautiful girl the other day
She was wearing triple heart earrings
And she had on a beautiful heart blouse too
She also had on a beautiful scarf
I thought, you go girl, look at you
She had a special day
And she said, I will continue to dress this way
Triple heart earrings, keep on doing what you do
And always remember that Jesus loves you

CONFIDENT WALK & CONFIDENT TALK

There's a beautiful lady that I see almost every day
She has a confident walk I must say
She likes to wear her high heel shoes
And also she wears pretty clothes too
She not only has a confident walk
But she is also confident in the way that she talks
Confident walk and confident talk, you are very special this is true
And always remember that Jesus loves you

BLUE JEANS AND JEAN DRESS

I saw a little baby a few weeks ago
She was very cute don't you know
Her mommy dressed her in cute little jeans and a cute little vest
She was definitely dressed to impress
Blue jeans and vest, keep on looking cute like you do
And always remember that Jesus loves you

BIRTHDAY SIGN

I met a lady a while ago
She was very beautiful don't you know
She was at the table working on some letters
I thought, I wonder what she is doing, that looks pretty clever
She told me that she was working on a birthday sign
She had a special person in mind
She was making it for a little kid
There was a big surprise party being thrown for him

The next day I asked her if he liked his sign
She said yes but he was kind of shy
Anyway that was a little while ago
And he still has his sign don't you know
Thanks for being so kind
Anyone should want to have a friend like you
You care a lot about people you really do
Birthday sign, keep on sharing kindness like you do
And always remember that Jesus loves you

BIRTHDAY JEWELRY

My coworker had some special jewelry from her mom
So on my birthday last year she brought me some
Pearl earrings and other precious jewels
Butterfly pin and a beautiful blue diamond broach pin
And beautiful necklaces too
It really touched my heart that she was so kind
And also that she's a friend of mine
Birthday Jewelry, thanks for being a blessing to me
I appreciate you
And always remember that Jesus loves you

BEAUTIFUL RED AND BLACK BUSHY HAIR

I met a lady a couple weeks ago
She was very beautiful don't you know
She had some of the most beautiful big bushy red hair
I really liked it I declare
Now she has changed it to black
It still looks good as a matter of fact

Then one day I heard her singing
I stopped her and asked her to sing for me
When she opened her mouth and began to sing
She just about blew me away, yes she did her thing
I told her that she belonged on The Voice
She would definitely be my first choice

Then she told me that she once sang for the president
I thought, wow we have a star in our midst
She also loves to write like me
We have a lot in common I see
She went to school to develop her beautiful voice
Wow she made such a good choice
Beautiful red and black bushy hair
Keep on doing the great things that you do
And always remember that Jesus loves you

PRETTY NECKLACE RC

I saw a beautiful lady in the dining room last week
She was a real cutie, then I looked at her neck and what did I see?
A beautiful necklace in front of me
When I got closer she just so happened to be a new RC
Pretty, pretty, pretty, yes indeed
Pretty necklace RC, Keep on looking beautiful like you do
And always remember that Jesus loves you

COOL HAIRCUT

I met a young man a while ago
He was very handsome don't you know
He had a haircut with an amazing design
Oh he is so handsome and fine
Always keep a good attitude
Your mom loves you and she cares about you too
And she always makes sure that you look good too
Cool haircut, keep on looking cool like you do
And always remember that Jesus loves you

KIND-HEARTED MAN

There is a man who works at my job
I see him almost every day
He has a very kind heart
And a soft smile upon his face
He loves working with people who are hurting
And encourages them along the way
He is very thankful for his job every single day
Kindhearted man, thanks for all that you do
And always remember that Jesus loves you

LEOPARD PANTS

I saw a lady walking down the hall today
She was very beautiful I must say
Then I looked at her pants and to my surprise
She had leopard prints on every side
I told her that her leopard pants are really cute
And she said, thanks I have them in purple too
Leopard pants, keep on looking cute like you do
And always remember that Jesus loves you

BEAUTIFUL WHITE FLOWING DRESS

I saw a lady the other day
She was very beautiful I must say
She had on a beautiful white flowing dress
And beautiful bling sandals too
I thought, wow you are really looking good
It looked like she was going to walk on the white carpet
To get an Oscar award
White flowing dress, you already won the Oscar to me
Because you are pretty, pretty, pretty yes indeed
White flowing dress, keep on looking beautiful like you do
And always remember that Jesus loves you

BLUE & WHITE MATCHING SWEATER AND TENNIS SHOES

I saw a lady the other day
She was very beautiful I must say
She had on a beautiful blue sweater with matching shoes
Wow that day she was really looking cool
Even though in her life she may be going through a lot
She still thinks on positive thoughts
I love talking to her every day
She always sends encouragement my way
Blue and white sweater and matching tennis shoes
Keep on looking beautiful like you do
And always remember that Jesus loves you

CUTE AND SWEET

There is a lady I see almost every day
She is cute and sweet I must say
She has some of the prettiest clothes
That I have ever seen
And she always looks so fresh and clean
And oh your white coat with the fur
Really looks good on you too
You really dress pretty, yes you do
Cute and sweet, stay focused in all that you do
And always remember that Jesus loves you

SMILES FROM GOD

A beautiful lady introduced me to her daughters the other day
They were very beautiful I must say
When I said hi to them their faces lit up with a smile
I just had to stand there and talk to them for a while
There was such a joy in those children, it was so evident to see
I could feel it in my heart yes indeed
It was like their smiles from God were just for me
Smiles from God, keep on smiling like you do
And always remember that Jesus loves you

HEROIC ACT

It was raining hard one day
You could hardly see anything
When all of a sudden a girl tried to run across the street
A car hit her and knocked her down
No one saw her but my friend
So she jumped out of her car and ran to her side
She helped her up to see if she was all right
Then she took her to the school nurse right away
To make sure that nothing was broken and she was okay
It just so happened the girl was fine
I would say that she was very fortunate
Because she could have died
Heroic act, thanks for the kind things that you do
And always remember that Jesus loves you

BLACK AND BURGUNDY HAIR

Black and burgundy is a beautiful color for you
But no matter what color your hair is
I'm sure it would look good on you
It's the beauty in you that radiates from your heart
I noticed this about you from the very start
Whether you have on sweatpants and a headband
Or whether you dress elegant like you do
There is still an inner beauty that radiates from you
Black and burgundy, keep on looking beautiful like you do
And always remember that Jesus loves you

GREEN PURSE AND GREEN SWEATER

I saw a lady a while ago
She was very beautiful don't you know
She had on a beautiful green sweater
And she had a pretty green purse too
And to top it off she had a beautiful hairdo

Then I started seeing her again and again
She always gives me a smile she's like a special friend
And by the way your son is very handsome too
I can see that he gets his good looks from you
Green purse and green sweater, you're amazing this is true
And always remember that Jesus loves you

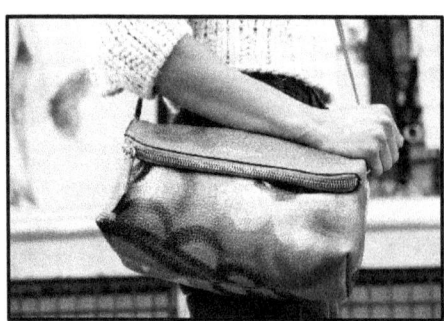

TOGETHER WITH BEST FRIEND

I saw a new lady today
She is very beautiful I must say
She just so happened to see one of her best friends
They laughed and hugged each other over and over again
I thought, wow that was so special to see
I'm going to write about this in my book for a good memory
She also had some of the most beautiful wavy hair
I really like it I declare
Together with your best friend
Encourage each other to make it through
And always remember that Jesus loves you

FLOWERED TATTOO

I met a new lady the other day
She was very beautiful I must say
She had a tattoo with beautiful lilies on her arm
And her kids' names too
I thought, wow that's an amazing tattoo
And you're very amazing too
You're beautiful like your flowers
And I'm sure your kids are very beautiful too
Be encouraged, flowered tattoo
And always remember that Jesus loves you

FLOWERED HAT

I saw a little girl a while ago
She was very cute don't you know
She had on a very cute flowered hat
She made me smile as a matter of fact
Her mom is also very beautiful
I could see that she gets her good looks from her
Flowered hat, keep on looking cute like you do
And always remember that Jesus loves you

COLORFUL FLOWERS AND BUTTERFLIES

I met a lady the other day
She is very beautiful I must say
I loved her sweet little smile
And her great personality too
And her shirt was so amazing
It had colored flowers and butterflies too
Colorful flowers and butterflies, you are amazing this is true
And always remember that Jesus loves you

DOUBLE TUTU

I was in the serving window the other day
When I saw a beautiful display
A little girl had a tutu on
And on her shirt there was a tutu too
Oh it was so amazing and cute
Yes, I got inspired so I made her another poem
I thought, double tutu is what I will call you
Double tutu, keep on looking cute like you do
And always remember that Jesus loves you

RED HOODIE

I met a young lady the other day
She was very beautiful I must say
She had on a red hoodie, my favorite color
And she was very kind, you just got to love her
She had a great smile on her face
Like she was really happy to be in this place
Red hoodie, keep on sharing kindness like you do
And always remember that Jesus loves you

VALENTINE'S PANCAKE LUNCH

On Valentine's Day
The woman and children were very happy I must say
My friend made them yummy pancakes
With a spread of strawberries, blueberries
Cool whip, and chocolate chips too
Butter and syrup is always an option
But on that special day
They had other yummy things they could choose
On that day when many feel alone
God touched my friend's heart to make them feel special that day
With their yummy pancake lunch
On their special Valentine's Day

MY SPECIAL FRIEND

You always took time to talk to me
And you were very special to me
Your voice was always so nice and soft
I liked how you always gave me a smile
And sometimes we just talked
I miss you and your little girl a lot
Many times you are in my thoughts
Whenever you read this book
I hope that it brings encouragement to you
My special friend, you and your daughter are so beautiful
And always remember that Jesus loves you

SURVIVOR

Your story is really amazing to me
You are a survivor I can see
If anyone wants to know if miracles come true
They can listen to your story and see, wow, yes it's true
The shirt you wear with "love" written on it is a good one for you
It should remind you how much God loves you
And He cares about you too
I believe that I am here to encourage you
And to help you have hope no matter what you're going through
This poem comes from the heart of God above
He wanted me to share this with you to remind you of His love
Survivor, you can do it, I believe in you
And always remember that Jesus loves you

CUTE BUN IN HER HAIR

There's a beautiful lady that I met the other day
She had a cute bun in her hair
And a beautiful smile upon her face
I really enjoy talking to her
There is something very special about her
She also has a cute colorful bag with pencils and pens
She is always prepared no matter what or when
Cute bun in her hair, keep on looking cute like you do
And always remember that Jesus loves you

FANTASTIC SHOES

I met a lady the other day
She was very beautiful I must say
She had a beautiful smile
That you could see for a mile
And she had nice shiny sunglasses
That really complemented her face
As I walked down the hallway with her
I just happened to look at her feet
She had the most fantastic colorful shoes
I liked them so much
I would like to have some of those shoes too
You go girl, I see that you have good taste
You're one of the coolest girls in this place
Fantastic shoes, keep on looking cute like you do
And always remember that Jesus loves you

BLUE-EYED RC

I met a lady one day when I was in the dining room
She was very kind and caring and very beautiful too
The two things that I remember most about her
Was her blue eyes and beautiful blonde hair
Yes she was amazing I declare
Yes a smile can go a long way
When someone gives it in a genuine way
Blue-eyed RC, keep on being kind in everything that you do
And always remember that Jesus Christ loves you

GOLDILOCKS HAIR

I met a girl the other day
She had Goldilocks hair and a beautiful face
She had her hair up, then she put it down
Her curls begin to bounce, bounce, bounce,
She is known for her beautiful hair
She is blessed, blessed, blessed I declare
She also has a good attitude whenever I talk to her
Goldilocks hair, I enjoy talking to you
And always remember that Jesus loves you

STRAWBERRY PAJAMAS

I saw a girl the other day
She was very beautiful I must say
She had on the cutest pajama pants
With strawberry patches all over them
I told her I liked her strawberry pants
She said thank you and smiled over and over again
Strawberry pants, I appreciate the kindness that I receive from you
And always remember that Jesus loves you

BONITA RC

I met a new lady today
She was very beautiful I must say
She had long black flowing hair
And a beautiful smile I declare
I ask her if she was Hawaiian
Because she looked like she was from a beautiful island
She said no she was Mexican
I said, okay Bonita then
Bonita RC, it was nice meeting you
And always remember that Jesus loves you

BLUE EYES AND NIKE SHOES

I met a little boy a while ago
He is very handsome don't you know
I love his beautiful blue eyes
And his Nike shoes are pretty cool too
His mommy always dresses him cool
He loves her and she loves him too
Blue eyes and Nike shoes, keep on looking cool like you do
And always remember that Jesus loves you

BLACK LACE VEST

You look beautiful, yes you do
I'm always amazed at what you wear
And how good everything looks on you
I love your black lace vest and your black lace shoes too
You really got a lot of style, yes you do
Black lace vest, keep on looking beautiful like you do
And always remember that Jesus loves you

TEEN RC CHEERLEADER

When I was thinking about a name to call you
Teen RC cheerleader seemed so fitting for you
You enjoy seeing the teens grow
And you keep on working with them even when they say no
You believe in the mission at our workplace
And I believe that you're very happy to be in this place
I always enjoy talking to you
And I like your sweet personality too
Teen RC cheerleader, keep on doing the good job that you do
And always remember that Jesus loves you

PARTY THROWER

I met a lady the other day
When I was eating in the dining room
She was throwing a special surprise party
For some pretty pregnant ladies
The cake was yellow trimmed in red
With colorful confetti

She wanted them to know
That she loved them all so much
And how she was glad
To work with such a wonderful bunch
They were very happy and surprised
My heart was so touched I almost cried
Party thrower, keep on doing the kind things that you do
And always remember that Jesus loves you

FLOWER FLOWING DRESS

I saw a lady the other day
She was very beautiful I must say
She had on a flower flowing dress
And her hair also looked lovely, it never looks a mess
I told her she looked beautiful and I was going to make her a poem
Then she smiled and went away
We had a great conversation that day
Flower flowing dress, keep on looking beautiful like you do
And always remember that Jesus loves you

HELLO KITTY SHIRT

I saw a little girl the other day
She was very beautiful I must say
She had on a Hello Kitty blouse
And some cute Nike tennis shoes
Her mommy dressed her really nice
Yes she was looking good
Hello Kitty shirt, keep on looking cute like you
And always remember that Jesus loves you

INSPIRING LADY

All of your children are beautiful
I can see that they get their good looks from you
Children become like the people they hang around
They will be great in this world
Because they have a wonderful mother like you
I love seeing you every day and by the way
I love your new hair color too
Thanks for always being kind to me
And always remember that Jesus loves you

PURPLE SWEAT SUIT

I met a lady last week
She was very beautiful and sweet
She had her hair up in a cute bun
And she also had a beautiful purple sweat suit on
She really looked cute I thought, you go girl, look at you
My mom would have loved your sweat suit
Purple was her favorite color and she looked good in it too
Purple sweat suit, keep on looking cute like you do
And always remember that Jesus loves you

EAGLE T-SHIRT

I met a beautiful lady the other day
She had on a beautiful eagle T-shirt
And she had a very beautiful face
We saw each other again in the hallway and we both said hi
Then we both smiled and went bye, bye
Eagle T-shirt, thanks for the kindness I receive from you
And always remember that Jesus loves you

SHOWER FROM THE LORD

One day I let my friend outside to take out some trash
The bag was torn and leaking so it was really a mess
When she came back in I asked her if she needed to take a shower
She said I got a shower from the Lord so why should I even bother
She laughed and I laughed too
Then she went away and I went back to eat my food
Shower from the Lord, I appreciate the humorous personality
That God has given to you
Keep on sharing kindness like you do
And always remember that Jesus loves you

MENTAL HEALTH THERAPIST

You have an amazing job yes you do
And your job is very important too
You help people with troubled minds get back on track
You fill in the gap where there is lack
You are beautiful this is true
Mental health therapist, keep on doing the good job that you do
And always remember that Jesus loves you

PINK GLITTER TENNIS SHOES

I met a lady some time ago
She was very beautiful don't you know
She had on a very pretty top
And a pair of pink glitter tennis shoes that really topped it all off
Yes, she was looking pretty cool
I knew it and she did too
Pink glitter tennis shoes, keep on looking cute like you do
And always remember that Jesus loves you

PLAID SHIRT AND SMOOTH HAIR

I saw a little baby boy in the dining room the other day
He is really handsome I must say
He had on a cool plaid shirt and some nice pants
And he also had plaid on the end of them
And oh his hair looked so nice and smooth
I thought, you go little baby, you're looking really cool
Plaid shirt and smooth hair, keep on looking cool like you do
And always remember that Jesus loves you

PRESCHOOL TEACHER

You are a beautiful preschool teacher
And you're very sweet too
I love seeing you're smiling face
And I appreciate your wonderful attitude
You love working with the children
And they also love learning from you too
You have been involved in education
Of young children for over 25 years
You have experience in special education too
You are one amazing young lady, that says a lot about you

You, have a bachelor's in education services
From Grandview University
You encourage everyone that comes around you
Children brighten your day
And you love to educate them too
When I see you reading to them
You make me want to sit down and listen too
You love exercising, biking, and spending time with your family too
You have two daughters and I'm sure they are as beautiful as you
Preschool teacher, keep on doing what you do
And always remember that Jesus loves you

ROSE TATTOO

I met a lady a few days ago
She is very beautiful don't you know
She had a rose tattoo on her arm that was pretty cool
When I talked to her she had a smile on her face
That said, hello how are you
And I hope that you have a good day
She has a very contagious smile
It's not fake, it lasts for a while
She encourages everyone she sees
I have happy thoughts about her
And so does everyone around her
Rose tattoo, keep on sharing your smile like you do
And always remember that Jesus loves you

INSPIRATIONAL SMILE

I saw a lady walking down the hallway the other day
She was very beautiful I must say
The thing that I remember most about her
Was her smile that said, hello world
Her smile was so inspirational to me
When I see her smile she makes me happy yes indeed

Then I saw her another day in the dining room
She had on some beautiful bling bling
And that same beautiful smile too
She had on a bling bling flower necklace
Sunglasses, and bling bling shoes too
I said, wow you are really looking good
Inspirational smile, you are such a blessing to me
Keep on being happy and free
And keep on smiling like you do
And always remember that Jesus loves you

BEAUTIFUL GRADUATING GIRLS

I saw two young ladies walking down the hallway one day
They were beautiful I must say
Then I came to find out that they were interns doing different jobs
They loved working with the kids
Most of all also they were graduating from Waukee High School
I thought, wow that's cool
Then I saw a picture of the blonde that was really cute
She had on an orange dress with a yellow flower in her hand
She was standing next to one of her graduating friends
Then I saw a picture of her friend that worked with her
She had on black pants a beautiful blouse and cute shoes
She was standing in front of a background
With colorful different shape balls
And she had a big smile on her face
You could tell that she was very happy that day

COLORFUL AND SWEET

There's a lady that I know
I met her a while ago
She always wears pretty colors
And pretty eyeshadow too
Her colors are usually bright
They remind me of springtime on a beautiful afternoon
And every time I see her
She is always sweet to me
God blessed me with a kind friend
He thinks a lot of me
Colorful and sweet, I appreciate you
And always remember that Jesus loves you too

CUTE HEADBAND AND PRETTY SHORTS

I met a young lady the other day
She was very beautiful I must say
She had on a cute headband and pretty shorts too
And she had a welcoming smile that said, hello, how do you do
Her mother is also very beautiful and young looking too
Later that day she had on a soft pretty pink robe
I could imagine being wrapped up in it when it's cold
Cute headband and pretty shorts, keep on looking cute like you do
And always remember that Jesus loves you

ANGEL WINGS

I was in the dining room today
When a beautiful lady came my way
I had to turn around and look at her again
She was so beautiful, like a breath of fresh wind
Then I looked at her back and what did I see?
Beautiful angel wings, oh they looked so heavenly
Oh it was such a good thing to see
It's like angels came down to visit me
She also had on a cute skirt with lace
She was one of the prettiest ladies in this place
Angel wings, keep on looking beautiful like you do
And always remember that Jesus loves you

LONG BRAIDS

I met a lady a little while ago
She was very beautiful don't you know
She had two long braids in her hair
I could imagine that I was a little girl
Swinging on her long braids
Playing outside in the fresh air without any cares
Long braids, keep on looking beautiful like you do
I also like the new color in your hair
It makes it look more beautiful I declare
You're an amazing lady this is true
And always remember that Jesus loves you

BLING BLING BUTTERFLY WATCH

I met a lady a while ago
She was very beautiful don't you know
She had on a bling bling butterfly watch
It was so cute it made me want to go shop
Bling bling butterfly watch
Keep on wearing cute things like you do
And always remember that Jesus loves you

COLORFUL SLEEPER & MATCHING BIB

I saw a beautiful baby in the dining room a while ago
Her mom always dresses her so pretty don't you know
She had on a colorful sleeper and a matching bib
She always looks so cute again and again
Colorful sleeper and matching bib, keep on looking cute like you do
And always remember that Jesus loves you

SWEATPANTS WITH A BLING BLING HEART

I saw a new lady the other day
She was very beautiful I must say
She had on sweatpants with a bling bling heart
I thought, those pants are amazing right from the start
I told her I really liked your pants
Then she said thanks and went on her way
I think I made her happy that day
Bling bling pants, keep on looking cute like you do
And always remember that Jesus loves you

TACOS AND TATTOOS

I met a lady a few day ago
She was very beautiful don't you know
She had some of the most amazing tattoos
And by the way she loves tacos too
We talked and laughed in the window for a while
Then she turned around and left with a smile
Tacos and tattoos, I really enjoyed talking to you
Keep the fun personality that I see in you
And always remember that Jesus loves you

COLORFUL CHEETAH PANTS

I saw a lady in the dining room the other day
She was very beautiful I must say
She had on some of the most amazing colorful cheetah pants
She looked like she was ready to go out and dance
I really liked her beautiful colors
She said that she also had some others
I could imagine wearing different color socks
And pretty bright tops
Then I could make up a song called the rainbow dance
With my colorful socks, top, and pants
Colorful cheetah pants, keep on looking cute like you do
And always remember that Jesus loves you

I APPRECIATE YOU

I know that you do a lot and you're good at what you do
But sometimes I know you get over whelmed
And you wonder, does anybody appreciate you
Well I just want you to know
Even though I don't directly work with you
I see how busy you are
And some of the responsibilities that are given to you
So keep your head up and keep on doing the good job that you do
I appreciate you
And always remember that Jesus loves you

MOTHER SINGING TO HER SON

I was getting the salad bar ready for supper one day
When I heard some music across the way
I turned around and to my surprise
A mother was singing to her son and she wasn't even shy
They were playing cards together, yes, they were having fun
She was very happy to be with her son
Mother singing to her son, keep on doing what you do
As your son gets older
He will remember those great memories with you
You're a very special young lady
And always remember that Jesus loves you

ONE OF THE PRETTIEST WOMEN IN THE WORLD

I met a teen RC some time ago
She looked like a beautiful model from a runway show
I saw her in the hallway again today
She still looked like a beautiful model I must say
She looks like a beauty queen
In someone's imagination that came alive
For all of us to see
Pretty, pretty, pretty as a picture
That's what you are to me
One of the prettiest women in the world
Keep on looking beautiful like you do
And always remember that Jesus loves you

PRETTY FACE AND TINY WAIST

I was in the serving room a few days ago
When I turned around I saw a beautiful girl don't you know
She has a very pretty face
And she also has a tiny waist
By the way her hairstyle is pretty cute too
I thought, you go girl, look at you
Pretty face and tiny waist
Keep on looking cute like you do
And always remember that Jesus loves you

RED AND WHITE ONESIE

When I walked down the hallway today
I saw a handsome baby boy, hey, hey, hey,
He had some amazing beautiful blue eyes
I stood there and looked at them for a little while
He had on a red and white onesie
All snuggled in his stroller seat
He was happy to be with his mommy
I'm sure it was a big treat
Red and white onesie
Keep on looking handsome like you do
And always remember that Jesus loves you

BLUE EYES AND PINK BIB

I saw a baby girl the other day
She was very beautiful I must say
She had some of the most beautiful blue eyes
That I have ever seen
And she had on a pretty pink bib
To keep her clothes clean
Her mommy was so happy to be with her little girl
You could tell that she was a big part of her world
Blue eyes and pink bib, keep on looking cute like you do
And always remember that Jesus loves you

GOOD MANNERS

I had another name for you
But good manners really describes you
You come to the window to get your food everyday
You're always kind and thankful and you never complain
You always have a smile on your face
Your warm fellowship I really embrace
The world is a great place because you're here my dear
Good manners, I appreciate you
Keep on showing a good example like you do
And always remember that Jesus loves you

STRIPED HOODIE

I saw a lady the other day
She was very beautiful I must say
She had a beautiful striped hoodie on
And a cute haircut too
I looked at her and thought
You go girl, beautiful you
She also had a great personality
Which is very special to me
Striped hoodie
Keep on looking beautiful like you do
And always remember that Jesus loves you

SOCCER TATTOO

There's a lady with long flowing hair I met a couple of years ago
She is very beautiful don't you know
She has a soccer ball tattoo on her arm and her son's name too
She's a very special lady and she has a great personality too
Soccer tattoo, keep on looking beautiful like you do
And always remember that Jesus loves you

MOONLIGHT PANTS

I was in the dining room one day
When all of the sudden a beautiful young lady came my way
She had on some amazing moonlight colored pants
They reminded me of the science center when I was a kid
They looked pretty comfortable
I wouldn't mind having a pair of them
Moonlight pants, keep on wearing cool pants like you do
And always remember that Jesus loves you

LOVE TANK TOP

*Your love tank top and your beautiful red hair with a cute ponytail
Are the first two things that I noticed about you
And your smile is very contagious too
I smiled right away when I looked at you
And you also have a great personality too
These are some of the nice things that I thought about you
Love tank top, keep on looking beautiful like you do
And always remember that Jesus loves you*

POEM FOR ME

*Even though it's short, it's very sweet
You make me laugh, yes indeed
I read my poem often when I'm writing in my room
You encourage me a lot, you really do
Thanks for taking time to write to me
I know many times your schedule is very busy
I also have a busy schedule too
But we must take time to encourage people like we do
Keep doing the good job that you do
And always remember that Jesus loves you*

TIE DYE SHORTS WITH RUFFLES

*I met a lady the other day
She was very beautiful I must say
She had on some tie dye shorts with ruffles that were really cool
I thought, you go girl, look at you
Tie dye shorts, keep on looking cute like you do
I appreciate the kindness that I receive from you
And always remember that Jesus loves you*

SALSA DRESS

I saw a lady the other day
She was very beautiful I must say
She had on a beautiful salsa dress with pretty colors
I told her that her dress was pretty
And many other people told her the same thing too
She smiled and went happily on her way
I believe that we made her happy that day
Salsa dress, keep on looking beautiful like you do
And always remember that Jesus loves you

DREAMY EYES

I met a lady the other day
She was very beautiful I must say
She had some of the dreamiest blue eyes that I have ever seen
When I looked at her face I started to dream
Of the beauty that I saw in her
Your eyelashes and your eyeshadow
Really bring out the beauty in you
And your bling bling earrings are beautiful too
Let's not forget your fingernails that match your bracelets too
You really got it going on, yes you do
Dreamy eyes, keep on looking beautiful like you do
And always remember that Jesus Christ loves you

BLUE BANDANA DRESS

I saw a little girl some time ago
She was very beautiful don't you know
But the thing about her that really caught my eye
Was that she was wearing a blue bandana dress
And it looked pretty fly
Also she looked like her mom
She could pass for her twin
Beautiful bandana dress, keep on looking cute like you do
And always remember that Jesus loves you

AMAZING TATTOO

I met a lady the other day
She had some amazing tattoos
And a beautiful face
Her tattoos say blood makes you related
And loyalty makes you family
I'm loyal to fix you food
So I consider myself part of your family too
I love your great personality
And your good conversations too
I really look forward to getting to know you
Amazing tattoos, keep on looking beautiful like you do
And always remember that Jesus loves you

BLONDE HAIR AND BLUE STRIPES

I met a lady a few days ago
She is very beautiful don't you know
She has blonde hair with blue stripes
Actually it looks pretty nice
She also wore many bracelets too
They were kind of big but pretty cool
Blonde hair and blue stripes
Keep on looking beautiful like you do
And always remember that Jesus loves you

FINE YOUNG MAN

I was in the serving room the other day
When I gave a young man his plate
He was as fine as they come
And his mom was also a beautiful one
Another thing that I noticed about him
He was also fine in his mannerism
He treated his mom with much respect
Wow his mom sure did a good job raising him
You could tell by the way that he is
Fine young man, keep on respecting your mom like you do
And always remember that Jesus loves you

KINDNESS DISPLAYED

When I look at your face what do I see?
Kindness, kindness, looking back at me
Your smile comes from heaven above
When you smile at people you display God's love
You're beautiful, beautiful, this is true
And always remember that Jesus loves you

COLORFUL DRESS

*I was in the hallway the other day
When a beautiful girl walked my way
She had on a beautiful colored dress
And colorful sparkled tennis shoes
She was looking very happy that day
She looked like a colorful display
Colorful dress, keep on looking cute like you do
And always remember that Jesus loves you*

EYESHADOW AND MATCHING SWEATER

*There's a lady I see almost everyday
When she comes to the window
She always looks very pretty
The other day she had on a beige colored sweater
And eyeshadow that matched
She was really looking good and that's fact
Eyeshadow and matching sweater
Keep on looking beautiful like you do
And always remember that Jesus loves you*

MOMMY ROCKS T-SHIRT

*I saw a little boy some time ago
He had on a cute little T-shirt that said my mommy rocks
It would also be cute on a pair of socks
He was glad to be with his mom
And she was glad to be with her boy
You could tell that he was her pride and joy
My mommy rocks T-shirt, keep on looking handsome like you do
And always remember that Jesus loves you*

DRESSED UP TEEN

I was in the dining room one day
When a beautiful teen walked my way
She had on a beautiful black dress and long silky red hair
She was looking very pretty I declare
Dressed up teen, keep on looking beautiful like you do
And always remember that Jesus loves you

GREEN HOODIE WITH A BIT OF BLING

I came into the dining room the other day
There was a beautiful baby right in front of my face
She had on a green hoodie with a bit of bling
She was very precious yes indeed
Her mommy was very happy too
She was so glad to have her precious jewel
I talked to her baby and told her
She was a gift from God in heaven above
I touched her little hand and I felt God's love

MONSTER JAM TRUCK T-SHIRT

I met a new boy today
He is very handsome, hey, hey, hey
He had on a pretty cool shirt
With big trucks on the front
He said they're monster jam trucks
Well his shirt was a pretty color blue
And the trucks on his shirt were pretty amazing too
Monster jam truck T-shirt
Keep on looking handsome like you do
And always remember that Jesus loves you

THE BABY WHO LISTENS

I went into the dining room to take a break the other day
So I could meet a new lady and her baby
I sat down to let her know who I was
And so I could make a poem for her and her son
Her little baby just stared at me as he listened so closely
He really inspired me today
That's why I put him in my book, hey, hey, hey
The baby who listens, keep on being a good listener like you do
And always remember that Jesus loves you

PINK PUPPY SLEEPER

You look so cute yes you do
In your pink puppy sleeper, look at you
Your mommy loves, loves, loves you
You're all snuggled in your mommy's arms
Getting ready to go to sleep
In heavenly peace
Pink puppy sleeper, keep on looking beautiful like you do
And always remember that Jesus loves you

PEARL NECKLACE BLOUSE

I was in the window serving food today
When a beautiful lady came my way
She had beautiful blonde hair with beautiful curls
And a beautiful blouse adorned with pearls
Oh she looked so beautiful today
I had to look at her twice before she walked away
Pearl necklace blouse, keep on looking beautiful like you do
And always remember that Jesus loves you

BROWN FLOWING HAIR

I met a new lady in the dining room the other day
She has some of the most beautiful brown flowing hair
And she has a very pretty face
Her little boy is really handsome too
I thought, wow I can see that he gets his good looks from you
I really enjoy talking to you and your handsome son too
Brown flowing hair, keep on looking beautiful like you do
And always remember that Jesus loves you

LEOPARD ROBE

I saw a beautiful girl the other day
She had on a beautiful leopard robe, hey, hey, hey
I just had to touch it and see
If it was as warm as it looked to me
It was just as I thought
In time I will get me a robe like that too
So I can be nice and warm when I'm cold writing in my room
Leopard robe, keep on looking cute like you do
And always remember that Jesus loves you

PRETTY FACE AND PRETTY HAIR

I was in the dining room a while ago
When I saw a girl with a very pretty face
And she also had beautiful long hair too
She is very respectful and she has a great attitude
I love seeing her pretty face and I enjoy talking to her too
Your mom is also very special and she is very beautiful too
Pretty face and pretty hair, keep on looking beautiful like you do
And always remember that Jesus loves you

PINK AND GRAY AND CUTE HAIRSTYLE

*Pink and gray looks good on you
And your cute hairstyle also looks very beautiful too
I noticed your cute hairstyle when I first saw you
And also your beautiful jacket too
You're a very special young lady
And you have a great personality too
And always remember that Jesus loves you*

MIDNIGHT BABY GIRL

*I finally got to see the midnight baby girl
Her mommy held her tightly in her arms
I could see that she is a big part of her world
She had on a polka dot onesie and a cute blue bib
She had some of the prettiest black hair that I have ever seen
It was a special day for Mommy and her new baby
Midnight baby girl, keep on looking beautiful like you do
And always remember that Jesus loves you*

PINK AND WHITE BANDANA

*I sat across from a lady today
She had on a beautiful pink and white bandana
And her eyes were a beautiful brown color like mine
I could definitely relate
And by the way, she is one of the prettiest ladies in this place
I enjoyed talking to her and her son while I was on my break
I hope that I encouraged them by the kindness I displayed
Pink and white bandana, keep on looking beautiful like you do
And always remember that Jesus loves you*

JAPANESE BLOSSOM TATTOO

I saw a lady the other day
She had a cool Japanese blossom tattoo on her arm
And she also had other beautiful tattoos displayed
She had beautiful hazel colored eyes and pretty eyelashes too
I thought, you go girl, you are looking good
Japanese blossom tattoo, keep on looking beautiful like you do
And always remember that Jesus loves you

BLACK BLING BLING HEART

You look pretty every day
I really like your black bling bling heart
That is so beautifully displayed
And I really like your black hair too
You really know how to match, look at you
Black bling bling heart, keep on looking beautiful like you do
And always remember that Jesus loves you

HE LOVES CARS

I was in the window serving the other day
When a handsome boy and his mom came my way
He had cars in his hands, at least 2 or 3 of them
He reached out like he wanted me to play with them
I smiled as they left the window and went to sit down and eat
I thought, that was so kind of him, he is so sweet
He loves cars, keep on sharing your cars like you do
And always remember that Jesus loves you

BLANKET OF MANY COLORS

I met a lady the other day
She was very beautiful I must say
She was standing in the window
Wrapped up in something with beautiful colors
I told her, okay I will call your poem the blanket of many colors
She also had a beautiful smile on her face
I could tell that she was very happy to be in this place
She was very kind with good manners too
She always says thank you for her food
I don't know where you came from but I really like you
And I appreciate the kindness I receive from you
Blanket of many colors, keep on sharing kindness like you do
And always remember that Jesus loves you

DIAMOND NECKLACE SANDALS

I was in the dining room a little while ago
When I saw a beautiful lady in front of me
She just happened to be a teen RC
Then I looked down at her feet
Because something shinny caught my eyes
She had on diamond sandals
I got so excited and my voice got really high
Her sandals looked like diamond necklaces
Yes they were so amazing to me
Oh she looked so pretty, pretty yes indeed
Diamond necklace sandals
Keep on looking beautiful like you do
And always remember that Jesus loves you

MR. GREEN

I saw a boy in the dining room one day
He was very handsome I must say
He had on a light green top and some cool green shorts
And a smile on his face that said, hello world
I was trying to think of a name to call him that day
He said, call me Mr. Green, and I said okay
Mr. Green, keep on looking cool like you do
And always remember that Jesus loves you

BEAUTIFUL ASIAN LADY

I met a lady a while ago
She was very beautiful don't you know
She had some of the most beautiful two-toned color hair
Soft skin, beautiful teeth, and beautiful eyebrows I declare
She also had a very beautiful shape
She is one of the prettiest ladies in this place
I love working with her she's a great team player too
Beautiful Asian lady, keep on doing the good job that you do
And always remember that Jesus loves you

RED STRIPE BROTHERS

A beautiful lady's kids came to visit today
They are very handsome I must say
But the thing that I first noticed about the two of them right away
Was the red stripe they both had in their hair
I thought that it was pretty cool and smooth
Because my favorite color is red too
Red stripe brothers, keep on looking cool like you do
And always remember that Jesus loves you

REUNITED

*Reunited again I'm so happy for you it's like happy New Year
Happy Thanksgiving, and Merry Christmas all in one
To be together again with your precious sons
You have three precious gifts that God has given to you
Stay focused in everything that you do
You need your kids and they need you too
My heart rejoices with you
And always remember that Jesus loves you*

PRETTY CHAUFFEUR

*On the way home from a work meeting one day
A pretty chauffeur came our way
She greeted us with a big smile
And talked to all of us for a little while
She smiled from the time she picked us up
Until she dropped us off at work
I see her at work from time to time
I consider her as a friend of mine
Pretty chauffeur, keep on showing kindness like you do
And always remember that Jesus loves you*

MINNIE MOUSE FLOWER DRESS

*I saw a little girl in the dining room the other day
She had on a cute Minnie Mouse flower dress
With a built in bow in the back of her dress
And a yellow flower in her hair
She really looked cute I declare
Minnie Mouse flower dress, keep on looking cute like you do
And always remember that Jesus loves you*

HANDSOME PRIMARY COUNSELOR

I met a young man in passing a few months ago
Come to find out he is a primary counselor don't you know
He plans things for clients to get better
He loves his job and he loves people who are hurting too
Handsome primary counselor
Keep on doing the good job that you do
And always remember that Jesus loves you

BLUE AND BLACK HAIR

Your blue and black hair is really amazing to me
In reality it brings out your natural beauty
I always love seeing your face
And your kind personality I will always embrace
Stay here as long as you need to
We all care about you
And always remember that Jesus loves you

SOFT BROWN SILKY HAIR

I love your soft brown silky hair
And I also love your beautiful smile too
Your soft brown silky hair and your smile
Are the first two things I noticed about you
Let's not forget your great personality too
You have always treated me so kind
And I appreciate that about you
Soft brown silky hair, keep on looking beautiful like you do
And always remember that Jesus loves you

TEN YEAR COWORKER

*There is a lady that I have known for ten years
She is as beautiful now as she was back then
Whenever I see her she has a smile on her face
I believe that she is very happy to be in this place
Ten years—she seems like a dedicated person to me
She has a heart for people who are hurting, this I can see
She has a lot of compassion in her heart
I could tell that about her right from the start
Ten-year coworker
Keep on loving the women and children like you do
And always remember that Jesus loves you*

KEYCHAIN SECURITY GUARD

*There's a beautiful lady I have known for a while
She always says kind words to me
And she always has a smile
There's another thing special about her
She makes keychains of kindness in her spare time at work
The keychains helps us not to lose our keys
Because they are so bright and pretty
Keychain security guard
Keep on making those nice key chains like you do
I appreciate you
And always remember that Jesus loves you*

BLONDE AND BLUE

Wow It doesn't matter what color your hair is
Because you're still beautiful, beautiful
I liked it when it was blonde
Now I like it blue
Like I said it doesn't matter what color your hair is
You're still beautiful, beautiful, beautiful
Blonde and blue, keep on looking beautiful like you do
And always remember that Jesus loves you

AMAZING SKETCH ARTIST

When I went into the dining room today
I saw something that really amazed me
A beautiful lady was doing sketch art
As I went a little closer to see
I was really amazed at her creativity
She was drawing a picture of a forest with lots of grass and trees
I had seen something like this on TV, but not right before me
It was so alive I felt so energized
You're an amazing sketch artist this is true
You go girl, keep on doing what you do
And always remember that Jesus loves you

AMAZING HAIRSTYLE RC

Amazing hairstyle RC is what I think about when I look at you
And I also like your kind personality too
The teens are blessed to have a kind and caring RC like you
You really care about them, it shows in everything that you do
Amazing hairstyle RC, keep on sharing kindness like you do
And always remember that Jesus loves you

PRETTY RC FROM THE LAUNDRY ROOM

I was at work in laundry room one day
When a beautiful lady came my way
She had some of the prettiest hair that I have ever seen
And her blue eyes were also amazing
We were kind to each other that day
We both enjoy our job, hey, hey, hey
Pretty RC from the laundry room
Keep on enjoying your job like you do
And always remember that Jesus loves you

MICHAEL JORDAN SHIRT AND PANTS

I saw a handsome boy in the dining room today
He had a basketball player on his shirt
It was Michael Jordan, hey, hey, hey
Then I asked him if he liked basketball
And he said, yes and football too
He had Michael Jordan on his pant leg too
Michael Jordan shirt and pants, keep on looking cool like you do
And always remember that Jesus loves you

SNUGGLE BUGGLE

I saw a young lady last week
She had her little boy in her arms, oh he looked so sweet
He was snuggled close in his mother's arms
He felt secure and safe from harm
She had a smile on her face
As she gave him her motherly embrace
Snuggle buggle, your mom loves you, this is true
And always remember that Jesus loves you

CUTE AND CURLY

I met an RC a while ago
She is very beautiful don't you know
She has curly hair and a cute face
And a great personality that touches everybody in this place
Then yesterday I saw her again
She had on a beautiful patch colored jacket
That went well with her skin
Cute and curly, keep on sharing the great personality inside of you
I enjoy seeing you every day
And I appreciate the kindness that you display
You are a blessing here this is true
And always remember that Jesus loves you

HAWKEYES FAN

I met a lady the other day
She is very beautiful I must say
She had the word Hawkeyes in big logos
Written on her pants
I asked her if she liked the Hawkeyes
She got really excited and said, yes I'm a big fan
Hawkeyes fan, keep on loving the Hawkeyes like you do
And always remember that Jesus loves you

COLORFUL CAMERA SHIRT

I was in the dining room a few days ago
When I saw a beautiful lady eating with her kids
I walked over to the table and what did I see?
A beautiful little girl with a black tutu on
And a colorful camera shirt
It was so beautiful to see
It looked like rainbows were in front of me
She looked so beautiful yes indeed
Colorful camera shirt and black tutu
Keep on looking beautiful like you do
And always remember that Jesus loves you

PRETTY PURPLE DRESS

I saw a little girl one day with her mom
She had a very pretty purple dress on
She smiled as she walked with her mom down the hallway
She was beautiful just like her mommy I must say
I had to turn around and take a second look
They looked like twins
I wrote it down in my book
Pretty purple dress, keep on looking cute like you do
And always remember that Jesus loves you

BLACK LACE BLOUSE AND BLUE EYES

I was in the window serving food the other day
When a very beautiful lady appeared right before my face
She had some very gorgeous blue eyes
And a beautiful black lace blouse that caught everyone's eyes
I told her that I really liked her blouse
She smiled and turned to the side
Like she was a beautiful model that night
Lace blouse and blue eyes, keep on looking beautiful like you do
And always remember that Jesus loves you

PRETTY PREGNANT BLONDE RC

There's a lady I met a while ago
She is very pretty beautiful don't you know
I love her beautiful smile and her great personality too
She just happens to be a teen RC
And by the way she is pregnant too
She is always kind to me
And I really enjoy her company
Pretty pregnant blonde RC, thanks for all that you do
And always remember that Jesus loves you

I WILL MISS BOTH OF YOU

I talk to your baby just about every day
We have a bond together, I believe it's safe to say
One day you will be gone from here
And I will miss both of you
But I will always have found memories of you two
And always remember that Jesus loves you

STAR PLAYER

I met a guy a while ago
He is very handsome don't you know
He loves to play basketball and he loves to run track
He's very good at both of them as a matter of fact
He has some trophies for basketball and some ribbons for track
His mom and dad both encourage him, yes, they have his back
Star player, keep on doing the good job that you do
And always remember that Jesus loves you

BOARDS OF ENCOURAGEMENT

I was invited upstairs a few days ago
By a new lady I'm just getting to know
And to my surprise what did I see?
Boards of encouragement all around me
There were words of life yes indeed
Words of hope for you and words of hope for me
This lady does art and poetry
Just looking at the boards it is so plain to see
She definitely has a gift from God
For her inspiration we should give her an applause
Boards of encouragement
You're making a difference in everything that you do
And always remember that Jesus loves you

BEAUTIFUL FLAIR BLOUSE

I met a lady the other day
She is very beautiful I must say
She has very beautiful gray eyes
And some beautiful curly hair
And her flair blouse is also
Very beautiful and fancy I declare
But the thing I remember most about her
Was her pleasant attitude
I told her that I write books
She said that she also writes books too
Wow that really opened up a conversation between us two
Beautiful flair blouse, keep on looking beautiful like you do
And always remember that Jesus loves you

I'M GOING TO MISS YOU

I'm going to miss you talking to me
And always saying kind things to me
I'm going to miss seeing the beautiful clothes you wear
Especially your beautiful flowers
I'm going to miss you asking me what's for snack
I'm going to miss you telling me what happened in school
Like when you did a good job and won an iPad
I'm going to miss you, you are in my prayers
I pray that you make it out there
I'm going to miss you
I pray that great things happen for you
And always remember that Jesus loves you

RC WITH BEATLES SINGERS TATTOOS

I was in the waiting room the other day
When a beautiful lady came my way
I just so happened to look at her arm
I could see that she had a very colorful design
When I looked a little closer what did I see?
A picture of four Beatles singing superstars
The symbol of their band, a strawberry and vines
She really liked her tattoo but it took a lot of time
RC with the Beatles singers tattoo
Keep on looking cool like you do
And always remember that Jesus loves you

GLITTER EYELASHES & HIGH HEEL SHOES

I met a lady a while ago
She is very beautiful don't you know
She was all dressed up to go somewhere
She looked pretty cute I declare
She had glitter eyelashes and pretty hair
And some high heel shoes that were so cute
I thought, you go girl, look at you
I told her she looked good
She smiled like I knew she would
Glitter eyelashes and high heel shoes
Keep on looking cute like you do
And always remember that Jesus loves you

YOU LOOK LIKE MY GRANDDAUGHTER

I was amazed the first time I saw you
You look like my granddaughter, you really do
From your pretty smile to your long wavy hair
You're beautiful, beautiful, beautiful, I declare
I really like your beautiful T-shirt
And the positive words on it too
Congrats on your graduation to another grade
I pray that you do a good job in school
And always remember that Jesus loves you

RAINBOW AND STARS

I met a pretty lady the other day
She had beautiful rainbow and star tattoos
Oh they were so amazing and cool
Then I looked down at her feet
Hello Kitty slipper were right in front of me
I said, wow your slippers are really cool
She said, I don't just have pink ones but also blue
I said, you go girl, you're a cutie it's true
And always remember that Jesus loves you

COLORFUL HAIR AND EYESHADOW

Your hair is beautiful
And your eyeshadow is very beautiful too
I love your beautiful smile
And your great personality too
I always enjoy seeing you and talking to you too
You're a very special lady
And always remember that Jesus loves you

HAPPY LADY

A beautiful lady came to the window a little while ago
She was very happy don't you know
We had two of her favorite foods that day
She began to jump and shout hooray!
She was so happy she made us happy too
She was so happy to get our food
Happy lady, keep on being thankful for your food
And always remember that Jesus loves you

BUTTERFLY SHIRT AND PINK TUTU

I saw a little girl today
She looked very pretty I must say
She had on a cute little butterfly shirt and a cute pink tutu
I took a minute and talked to the little girl
And told her she looked so cute
She smiled and went with her mommy
As they walked down the hallway
Her pretty colors stayed in my mind most of the day
Butterfly shirt and pink tutu, keep on looking cute like you do
And always remember that Jesus loves you

GOLDEN EYES AND BEAUTIFUL SMILE

I saw a beautiful lady in the window one day
Her eyes looked golden, and she had a beautiful smile on her face
I thought, wow she's one of the prettiest ladies in this place
And whenever she talks to me she always has nice things to say
Golden eyes, keep on looking beautiful like you do
And always remember that Jesus loves you

MY HELPER

The other day I had two sauce pans
I tried to put them in the wells by myself
But they were too heavy for my hands
So I went into the dining room and asked a lady to help me
She didn't hesitate she came quickly
Because of her help everything went smoothly
Without her help it could have been a tragedy
Thank you my helper for being there for me
There is something very special about you
And always remember that Jesus loves you

HANDKERCHIEF SKIRT

I saw a lady in the serving room the other day
She had on a black and white handkerchief skirt
It is very, very pretty
She's so tiny she looks good in everything that she wears
Handkerchief skirt, keep on looking beautiful like you do
And always remember that Jesus loves you

LITTLE BEAUTY QUEEN

I saw a little girl a few days ago
She was really beautiful don't you know
She had on a cute pink tutu
And pretty pink hair bows in her curly hair
I told her mom she really looks so cute I must declare
Her mom told her to say hi, then she smiled and waved at me
I thought, wow she looks like a little beauty queen
I could picture her on a movie screen
Little beauty queen, keep on looking cute like you do
And always remember that Jesus loves you

ROSE COLORED PANTS

I love your rose colored pants and your beautiful blouse too
Everything that you wear always looks so good on you
You always take good care of yourself and your children too
That's what good mothers are supposed to do
Rose colored pants, keep on looking beautiful like you do
And always remember that Jesus loves you

ARROW DIAMOND EARRINGS

I was in the serving room the other day
When a beautiful lady came my way
She had some of the most beautiful arrow diamond earrings
That I have ever seen
And also some very beautiful white gold rings
Let's not forget her beautiful hair and face
She is definitely one of the prettiest ladies in this place
Arrow diamond earrings, keep on looking beautiful like you do
And always remember that Jesus loves you

COMPASSIONATE RC

Compassionate RC is what you are to me
You love the women and children with your whole heart
This everyone can see
You listen to them and you're there to help them
In any way that you can
You're also very special to me
And I think that you're very pretty
Compassionate RC, keep on showing compassion like you do
And always remember that Jesus loves you

HAPPY MOMMY

You're a happy mommy
And I'm sure your baby is very happy too
I love your beautiful smile every time that I see you
Your baby is a gift from God in heaven above
The way that you hold him is very evident of your love
Your smile is also a gift
Share it with everyone that you see
I'm sure your smile will be a blessing to everyone
I know your smile is a blessing to me
There is just something special about you
I look forward to getting to know you
And always remember that Jesus loves you

YOU LOOK LIKE A MOVIE STAR

When I saw you a few days ago
I thought, you look very familiar to me
You look like a beautiful lady that I saw in a movie scene
With long curly hair and beautiful skin
You were definitely born to win
Then when I got to meet you face to face
I thought you had one of the greatest personalities in this place
Well I hope you have fun in the job that you do
Even though at times it might be kind of challenging
But it's also very rewarding too
You look like a movie star, once again it was nice meeting you
And always remember that Jesus loves you

FOUR POUND MIRACLE BABY

Your baby is a miracle
That is very special to me
I was also a miracle baby too
Your baby weighed four pounds and I weighed three
Aren't we special, yes indeed
Your baby was born at just the right time
You will always remember how she helped save your life
Four-pound miracle baby
There is something special between me and you
Your mommy loves you very much
And Jesus loves you too

EIGHT MONTHS AND COUNTING

I met a lady the other day
She had on a pretty yellow T-shirt
And she had a very pretty face
Then later she told me that she was eight months pregnant
So eight months and counting is what I decided to call her
Pretty soon she will bring a wonderful gift into the world
Eight months and counting
I pray the best for you and your soon coming baby too
Be encouraged, we are here for you
And always remember that Jesus loves you

BABY CATCHER

It was a very special day, it was time for your niece to come
Your sister couldn't hold her any more
The doctor couldn't come fast enough
God had you in the exact right place
To be a catcher for your baby niece
On that special day she came into your precious arms
How awesome it must have felt to keep your niece from harm
As she came out right into your arms
Yes God had you be a catcher that day
What you did will forever stay with you
As your niece gets older you can share what happened with her too
Baby catcher, you are very special this is true
And always remember that Jesus loves you

YOU MAKE BEAUTIFUL BABIES

You make beautiful babies, this is true
It's not just a shirt that you wear, it's reality for you
You're beautiful and your children are very beautiful too
I love seeing your smiling face when you come to the window
Just seeing you smile makes me smile too
You make beautiful babies, enjoy your beautiful babies like you do
And always remember that Jesus loves you

NICE DRESSER WITH A SMILE

You always dress so nice and you always have a smile for me
I have known you for many years and you're always so kind to me
Nice dresser with a smile, keep on looking beautiful like you do
And always remember that Jesus loves you

GRATITUDE

When I looked up the word gratitude
There should have been a picture of you
Gratefulness, thankfulness, just happy to do what you do
You clean with a smile on your face
I can tell that you really enjoy what you do
Just being around you makes me feel good
You become like the people you hang around
I look forward to hanging around you
Gratitude, you're very beautiful and your son is very handsome too
I appreciate you and always remember that Jesus loves you

GIRAFFE WITH GLASSES ON

I was in the window a little while ago
When I saw a handsome boy don't you know
He had on a very unusual shirt
But it was a cool giraffe with glasses on
I had to look closer so I could see the amazing T-shirt right before me
Giraffe with glasses on, keep on looking cool like you do
And always remember that Jesus loves you

MOMMA'S HANDSOME SON

I saw a boy some time ago
He had on some nice shorts and a nice top too
He also had a nice short haircut too
I thought, wow you're really looking cool
Momma's handsome son, keep on looking cool like you do
And always remember that Jesus loves you

TREASURE CHEST POEMS

I saw a lady about a few weeks ago
She looked very familiar don't you know
She said, you made poems for me and my daughters years ago
I got so excited my face lit up with a big grin
So I said, do you still have them?
She said, yes they are in a treasure chest
I said, great that's what I hoped people would do
Put it in a treasure chest as a memory for you and your loved ones
To look back and see one day
And remember that someone loved you in a very special way
Treasure chest poems, hold on to your memories like you do
And always remember that Jesus loves you

FAMILY TIME UNDER A BEAUTIFUL TREE

When I got off work one day
I saw something that was so amazing to me
A beautiful family was spending time together on the grass
On a sunshiny day under a beautiful tree
There was not a better place they could have chosen that day
They had sunshine and a cool breeze
I thought to myself, how special
They are making great memories on a sunshiny day
Under a beautiful tree
Family time under a beautiful tree
Keep on making good memories like you do
And always remember that Jesus loves you

GHETTO STORY TATTOOS

I enjoy having a conversation with you
And I really like your amazing tattoos
They tell a story of your life in the ghetto
And how amazing you are too
Yes, you're a beautiful rose and I think that you're very special too
God's love is higher than any mountain and bigger than any ocean
I have made many mistakes
But every time I came back to God I received His amazing grace
God's love can heal all pain that is in our hearts
And if we trust in Him, He will and can give us a brand new start
Keep on trusting in God, remember that He has never left you
And always remember that Jesus loves you

YOU LOOK LIKE A TEENAGER

Though you're a little bit older, you still look like a teenager to me
And though sometimes you have to be strict in the job that you do
There is still a fun side of you
You look like a teenager to me
From your smiling face to your pretty curly hair
You look like a teenager to me I declare
Keep on doing the good job that you do
And always remember that Jesus loves you

DRESS OF MANY COLORS

I went to a meeting one day
When I turned around who did I see?
A beautiful lady in front of me
The thing about her that really caught my eyes
She had on a dress of many colors
She was looking really nice
Dress of many colors, keep on looking beautiful like you do
And always remember that Jesus loves you

PERSONALITY AND OWL TATTOO

I love your personality and also your owl tattoo
Owls are known to be wise and you're very wise too
I always enjoy seeing your face
And I appreciate your great attitude
You're beautiful like your mom and she is very wise too
Personality and owl tattoo, you're a blessing this is true
And always remember that Jesus loves you

MY CHEERLEADER FRIEND

You always give me a smile
And you always cheer for me
You were happy when I was talking about my books
And you're looking forward to hearing me sing
You said that you want to be a teacher when you grow up
I think that's a great career choice for you
My cheerleader friend, here's a cheer from me to you
You can do whatever you set your mind to do
And always remember that Jesus loves you

BLACK SWEATPANTS AND GOLD LETTERS

There's a lady I have known for a while
She is very kindhearted
And always greets me with a smile
She had some cute sweatpants on one day
With letters of love on her pant leg
I thought, wow your pants are really cool
You go girl, keep on looking cute like you do
Black sweatpants and gold letters, you're amazing this is true
And always remember that Jesus loves you

PART NINE: FAMILY AND COMMUNITY

GOOD LISTENER

She's sweet and kind
And she is an amazing student of mine
She does what I tell her to do
She never talks back
And she's never rude
She's a good listener for me
And she makes me very happy
Good listener, keep on doing good like you do
And always remember that Jesus loves you

NATIONWIDE VOLUNTEERS

I went to the daycare and what did I see?
Beautiful ladies all dressed in blue tees
They were nationwide volunteers, hey, hey, hey
They came to be a blessing and help with the children today
Also there were a few handsome men
You know we can't forget about them
Thank you nationwide volunteers for all that you do
And always remember that Jesus loves you

HOMEMADE GRILL CART

There's a man at my church who is very creative I must say
He made a homemade grill cart from scratch, hey, hey, hey
He has a table on his cart with a hole for a grill to fit in
And another grill on the side for more cooking
And he has a white fence around his cart to help everything stay in
Homemade grill cart, thanks for providing the grills
We appreciate you
And always remember that Jesus loves you

BELL SANDALS

I was in the Dollar Tree one day
When all of the sudden a pretty lady came my way
She had some very pretty curly hair
And a smile so bright you could see it anywhere
But the thing I remember most about her was her bell sandals
They jingled when she walked
I was so excited about her bell shoes
I told her that I was going to put her in my book
She said okay and we went our separate ways
Bell sandals, keep on jingling like you do
And always remember that Jesus loves you

MY FRIEND IN CHRIST

I went to praise and worship the other day
My friend looked really cute, hey, hey, hey
She had on some shinny gray boots
And cool black pants with the word faith
And a bling bling cross, I could see that she was making a stand
She wears some amazing things
She stands for Christ
And her singing voice is amazingly nice
My friend in Christ, keep on standing for Jesus like you do
And always remember that Jesus loves you

CHICAGO BULLS PANTS AND SPIDERMAN DRESS

I met a beautiful lady the other day
She was really cute I must say
She had on Chicago Bulls pants and a Spiderman dress
She looked really cute I must confess
Then I looked at her fingernails
Oh how she painted them all so well
One of them had a silver diamond clip
I thought, wow that girl is really hip
Chicago Bulls pants and Spiderman dress
Always remember that Jesus loves you the best

GOOD TO THE LAST DROP BANANA BREAD

One Wednesday night after class
My friend came in the room with a yummy looking snack
It looked so good I wish I had a bite
She told me there was more in the other room
So there I went zoom, zoom, zoom
I got there just in time
There were only a few pieces left
And I was hoping one of them was mine
A beautiful lady was there waiting for me
She gave me a piece of her yummy treat
I was so happy my tummy jumped for joy
It was so good I wished that I could have more
Good to the last drop banana bread
Keep on baking good like you do
And always remember that Jesus loves you

SURPRISE FROM MY HUSBAND

When I came home on Valentine's Day
I wasn't expecting anything
Because my husband and I don't usually celebrate
I went into my office and to my surprise
There was a beautiful array of gifts right before my eyes
A vase with flowers and hearts
Chocolate candy I wanted to eat right from the start
A beautiful glass rose in a box
And a fluffy heart that said I love you
There were other things too
I just thought I would share a few
I gave him a hug and said, thank you
That was a kind and caring thing for you to do
Husband I love you
And always remember that Jesus loves you too

LAUNDROMAT FRIEND

I met my friend about three years ago
We have become pretty close friends don't you know
I made her a poem one day
It really touched her heart I must say
We both believe in Jesus
That makes our conversation great
Because we know that He is the truth, the light, and the way
Laundromat friend, I appreciate you
And I really enjoy talking to you
You encourage me a lot, you really do
And always remember that Jesus loves you

PURPLE AND BLUE BUTTERFLIES

There's a lady at my church who is really sweet
And she always dresses so nice and neat
Last week she had on a black T-shirt
With purple and blue butterflies
She looked so pretty
She brought attention to my eyes
Purple and blue butterflies, keep on looking beautiful like you do
And always remember that Jesus loves you

INSPIRATION FLOWS OUT OF ME

Every day when I wake up inspiration flows out of me
It comes from my Heavenly Father you see
He knows that I'm faithful to do what He says
He inspires me before I even get out of bed

JESUS PAID THE PRICE FOR ME

Jesus paid the price for me, He died on the Cross at Calvary
Take the cross out of my songs is not an option for me
Jesus gave me life, He gave me eternity
How could you ask me to do such a thing?
My Lord Jesus Christ is the reason I sing
My songs of inspiration are from God above
Whenever I share a song I share His love
You see Jesus died on the cross and He rose again
Yes, He paid the price for all of my sins
I'm not ashamed to call Him my friend
He has been there with me through thick and thin
Take the cross out of my songs no way, no way!
The cross is a symbol of what He's done for me
And I will praise Him throughout all eternity
Jesus is the reason I'm alive today
Because of His grace and mercy
I'm not lying in my grave
No! No! I'm not ashamed of Christ
He's the reason why I live
He's the reason I have a life

NINETY-THREE-YEAR-OLD GRANDMA

There was a beautiful lady I used to know
She was 93 don't you know
She volunteered helping with babies
She loved rocking them in her arms
Keeping them safe from harm
She loved to wear a black leather jacket
And she also loved cooking too
I miss you ninety-three-year-old grandma
I always felt the love of Jesus through you

ANOINTED CHILDREN'S DIRECTOR

You're fun, loving, and very creative too
You care about the children a lot
It shows in everything that you do
They also get very happy
When they see you coming too
You sing with the children, bring them gifts
And also feed them too
Amazing children's director, I love you
Keep on doing the great job that you do
And always remember that Jesus loves you too

GOD'S ANOINTED NURSE

Countless people have been touched by you
I am one of them so I know it is true
You touch all of us with the kind words that you say
And also with the prayers that you pray
It's amazing even when you go through pain
You reach out to help others again and again
God's anointed nurse, you are beautiful inside and out
You love Jesus with all of your heart there is no doubt
God's nurse, keep on sharing love and compassion like you do
And always remember that Jesus loves you

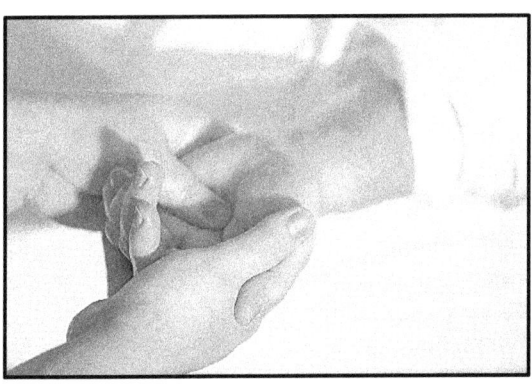

FAITHFUL SERVANT

There is a man that I have known for a few years
He is very kind and very sincere
He is faithful to help our pastors in any way he can
And he is always willing to lend a helping hand
Yes, he is faithful to God above
And he is quick to share his love
Faithful servant, keep on doing what you do
And always remember that Jesus loves you

TRUE HAPPINESS

Having the Lord in your life makes you truly happy
And very thankful too
You're right, everything else is a plus
When He's in the middle of everything you do
Just wait and trust in the Lord
And believe that He has a special someone for you
You're beautiful inside and out
It's like a beam of light shines out from you
True happiness, I pray the best for you
And always remember that Jesus loves you

SOUNDMAN

There's a very kind man I have known for a while
He comes to church ready to serve
His favorite job is doing the sound
He comes upon the platform to make sure that we can hear
He is faithful in what he does year after year
Soundman, thanks for all that you do
And always remember that Jesus loves you

SINGING STAR GIRL

There's a girl that I have known for a little while
She has a great personality and a beautiful smile
Even though she is kind of shy when she sings
She makes me smile again and again
The other day she had on a T-shirt with stars
I thought, that shirt represents who you are
Singing star girl, keep on looking beautiful like you do
And always remember that Jesus loves you

THE BATHTUB

The tub is a place where I can get away
And hear from my Heavenly Father
It is in those moments when we are together
That I can hear His voice speaking to my heart
Encouraging me not to fall apart
He gives me songs to encourage me
And countless others that I will see
I am thankful, thankful for my tub
But most of all for my Father's love

BLACK HAIR AND CUTE EYELASHES

There's a lady I have known for some time
I consider her as a friend of mine
She is so sweet and kind
She has some of the prettiest long hair
And cute eyelashes too
If you got to meet her for the first time
You would not only say that she's beautiful
But she's also fine too
Black hair and cute eyelashes
Keep on looking beautiful like you do
And always remember that Jesus loves you

PINK AND WHITE

Pink and white, pink and white
Oh you look so pretty tonight
Dressed in a little cute tutu
You have a beautiful bow in your hair
Pretty little white T-shirt
Two hearts in the middle of it too
And your name in the middle of one of the hearts
That is beautiful like you
And your cute little necklace that really complements you
Pretty French braids in your hair
And a beautiful crown too
Your mom and grandma love you so much
And Jesus loves you too
You won your first pageant and I'm so proud of you
Go girl, beautiful, beautiful you

FIVE-YEAR-OLD CARES FOR HIS MOM

My friend got sick the other day
And she had to go to the hospital right away
But first she had to pick up her 5-year-old from school
She had no choice he had to come
She was concerned he wouldn't listen, but to her surprise
He stayed there right by her side
He gave her water and asked her doctor if she was all right
Then he kissed her head as she lay down that night
He stayed there and helped her for five hours that night
The doctors couldn't believe that he was only five
Five-year-old, keep on helping your mom like you do
And always remember that Jesus loves you

ONE OF THE SWEETEST TEACHERS IN THE WORLD

I was at the laundromat a while ago
When I ran into my brother's grade school teacher don't you know
She was still as beautiful as she was years ago
Even though she wasn't my teacher I remember her well
She cared about all of the kids in school
And she made us mind her too
She spent 35 years teaching in public schools
She touched a lot of lives this is true
Wow I'm so amazed at the work that you do
Now 10 years in a Christian school
You teach, serve food, play outside with the kids
And even drive the van when you have to
You are such an amazing, beautiful lady this is true
I love you and always remember that Jesus loves you too

PURPLE AND GRAY

I was at Burger King and what did I see?
A beautiful lady with purple and gray hair on the other side of me
I said, wow I really like your hair
It was very pretty I declare
I told her, I'm going to make you a poem
She was so excited and her friends were too
It just goes to show you never know
Who you will run into
I didn't just make her a poem
I put her in my book
Her purple and gray hair inspired me
That's all it took
Purple and gray hair
Keep on looking cute like you do
And always remember that Jesus loves you

HOPE TO PEOPLE WHO FEEL HOPELESS

Many are down and out when they come to you
You share the same hope with them that was given to you
God has given you such love in your heart
You encourage people and give them hope
When they feel like they're going to fall apart
You see I am a witness, this is true
Many times God has spoken encouragement to me through you
God blesses everything that comes into your hands
Because He knows that He can trust you
Yes, you're His obedient man
So I hope that this poem encourages you
You mean a lot to all of us you really do
Hope to people who feel hopeless, keep on allowing God to use you
And always remember that Jesus loves you

BEAUTIFUL INSIDE AND OUT

You are so beautiful inside and out
We both love Jesus that's something to shout about
You are the apple of His eye and I am too
We must share the love of Jesus in everything we do
I watched you sing you did your thing
Anointed by God, yes you are a queen
We must keep moving forward to finish the race
Sharing God's love and His amazing grace
Beautiful inside and out, keep on doing what you do
And always remember that Jesus loves you

PRETTY FRESH FACE

When I looked at your picture what did I see?
A pretty fresh face looking back at me
I thought, wow you go girl, look at you
You look like a beauty queen out of a magazine, yes you do
I appreciate your kind heart and your great attitude
And I appreciate when you listen to me
Whenever I come and talk to you

HARD WORKER

There's a kind man I have known for a while
He loves to work at church and he always has a smile
Whether climbing on the roof to work or moping the floor
He's a hardworking man that's for sure
He is faithful in every way
He loves to give and he loves to pray
Hard worker, keep on being faithful in everything that you do
And always remember that Jesus loves you

RESTORED

The Lord restored you it's so evident to see
And you have such an amazing testimony
He gives you hope every day
And He has given you a new church family
At times you felt like you were on sinking sand
Now on Christ the solid rock you stand
Restored of the Lord yes this is true
In Him the possibilities are endless for you
You're an amazing man of God this is true
Thank you for working at church
We appreciate you
And always remember that Jesus loves you

BEDZZZ 4 LESS MAN

My husband and I went to Bedzzz 4 less today
We had such great customer service I must say
We were greeted with kindness after such a long day
Our bed will be delivered on Sunday
He even said I could relax in the bed
I wanted to, but I just sat on it instead
Before I left I told him I was going to put him in my book
Great customer service is all it took
Bedzzz 4 less man, thank you for the kindness
That we received from you
And always remember that Jesus loves you

RED WHITE AND BLACK DRESS

When I looked on my Facebook today
My sister-in-law had on a beautiful array
She had on a red, white, and black dress
She was definitely dressed to impress
Wow she always looks so cute
And also she is very intelligent too
And oh let's not forget about her hair
It always looks so cute anyway she wears it
Yes, she is one of a kind
I'm glad to have her as a sister-in-law of mine
Red, white, and black dress, keep on looking cute like you do
And always remember that Jesus loves you

WHITE LACE AND BLUE SUIT

I saw a beautiful lady on my Facebook page
She had on a beautiful white lace dress
And her hair was also beautifully laid in place
Next to her stood her prince charming in a blue suit
And he was very handsome too
He put his arm around her and kissed her
And she put her arm around him too
Oh how you make a very good couple, yes you do
Congrats on your third anniversary
I pray many more for you
And always remember that Jesus loves you

A NIGHT TO REMEMBER

February was a special night
I was all dressed up and I had a big appetite
We were on our way to church you see
There was a Valentine's dinner
Prepared for me and other church ladies
We were serenaded by candlelight
Waiters brought us a spaghetti dinner with salad and bread
And then we had some non-alcoholic grape juice delight

Then it was time for yummy cheesecake dessert
Then our pastor spoke up and reminded us of our worth
Then there was a drawing for three prizes
And two wonderful people entertained us with a wonderful skit
We really had fun, yes we did
We have pastors who care about us
They speak the truth and share God's love
We are all God's children and we are special to Him
Through Jesus Christ we always win!

BLACK AND YELLOW

Wow you both look amazing, this is true
Black and yellow really looks good on you two
You both look like models that's for sure
Then I looked down and saw your yellow boots
And his yellow shoes
And I thought, wow you both look so cool
But the one thing that is really amazing to me
Is how you treat each other so respectfully

You both love Jesus
That's the secret of your success
He is in the center of your marriage
That why you're both so blessed
God woke me up with both of you in my heart
So I wrote this down
So my memory wouldn't depart
I am so proud of you two
And always remember that Jesus loves you

THANKS FOR INTRODUCING ME TO MY SPIRITUAL MOM

You introduced me to a lady who has helped change my life
I will forever be grateful to you every day of my life
She spoke many prophecies in my life
And until this day they are still coming true
You have a part in every book and song
Because you were obedient that day
I love you and appreciate you too
And always remember that Jesus loves you

THREE BEAUTIFUL AFRICAN QUEENS

I looked at my friend's Facebook one day and what did I see?
Three beautiful African queens right before me
They had some of the most beautiful African dresses on
They were full of color, it was so beautiful to see
They looked like they had just taken beautiful pictures
From a photo shoot that day
And their lovely pictures were on display
Three African queens, keep on looking beautiful like you do
And always remember that Jesus loves you

GOOD SMELLING MAN

You're a good smelling man
And you are very handsome too
I remember in school I had a crush on you
At the time you were my boyfriend
And I loved looking at you
Now you're my husband
And I'm so glad I'm still with you

GIFTED MUSICIAN

*God taught you how to play the organ
And you didn't even have a lesson
You trusted God
And you kept your confession
God uses you in amazing ways
You play by ear and you begin to sing
A lot of my inspiration comes from you
If you can trust God I can too
Keep on listening to God, great things await you
And always remember that Jesus loves you*

SHE LIKES SCHOOL

*I met a young lady three years ago
She is very beautiful don't you know
She volunteered at our job helping her mom
She was such a blessing all day long
I asked her if she liked school and she said, yes I do
I was surprised to see a teenager in this day and age
Who loves to go to school and has a big smile upon her face
She likes school, keep on enjoying school
And always remember that Jesus loves you*

RAY OF SUNSHINE

When I think of you I think of the sunshine in the sky
It gets brighter and brighter as the day goes by
Many times when there was darkness in my life
God sent you to be a ray of sunshine
Wait a minute, you're not only a ray of sunshine to me
But to everyone you see
May God bless you in every area of your life
And once again thanks for being my sunshine
You are beautiful this is true
And always remember that Jesus loves you

COOL AND SMOOTH

I met a man the other day
He was cool and smooth I must say
He loves to listen to his music while he's at work
And he is kind to all of his customers as he rings us up
He was there when the store was first built
And he is still their today
He is a very hard worker I must say
Cool and smooth, keep on doing the good job that you do
And always remember that Jesus loves you

BLING BLING TOE SANDALS

I was at church a while ago
And my friend had on some bling bling toe sandals
I thought they were really cool
I said, you go girl, you're looking good
Bling bling toe sandals, keep on looking beautiful like you do
And always remember that Jesus loves you

KIND STORE MANAGER

I met a kind lady some time ago
She just happened to be a store manager don't you know
She always greets me with a smile
And when I was going through
She even stopped and listened to me for a while
She really cares a lot about her store
And she's a kind and caring boss, who could ask for more
Kind store manager, I appreciate you
And always remember that Jesus loves you

MY YOUNGEST GRANDSON'S MOM

My youngest grandson's mom is really beautiful
And her smile is really beautiful too
She has the most beautiful bouncy, curly red hair I have ever seen
And she has a great personality too
You're a wonderful mom and you're good to my son too
I really enjoy your company and I enjoy seeing you at church too
You're a very special young lady
And always remember that Jesus loves you

HANDSOME WIRE GUYS

There were some guys that came to work at my job
They worked really hard and they did a good job
They had to put a new fire system in
It was time for a new upgrade and that they did
Thanks guys, for helping us be safe
Handsome wire guys, you're really good at what you do
And always remember that Jesus loves you

BIRTHDAY CLOTHES

I was really blessed on my birthday this year
I received lots of presents and lots of birthday cheer
And oh to my surprise when I looked down what did I see?
A big bag of beautiful clothes just for me
I thought, oh my what do I have here
As my eyes began to fill with happy tears
My boss blessed me with nice warm clothes
How much they cost her, only God knows
But beyond that
She is kindhearted and that's a fact

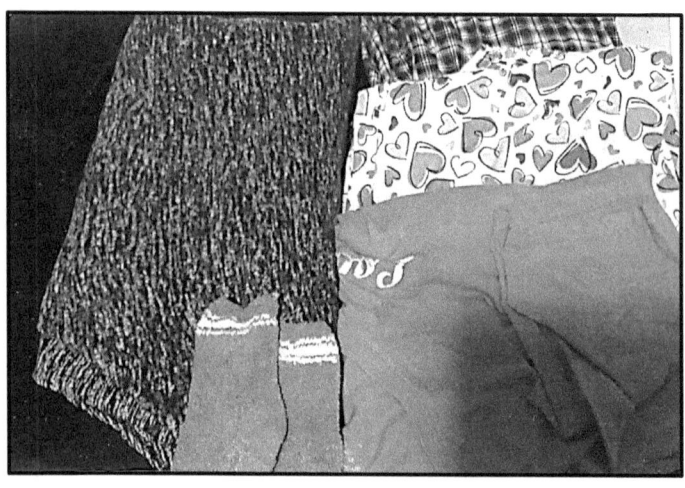

TWO PRETTY BRAIDS

I met a young lady at the laundromat today
She is very beautiful I must say
She has two beautiful long braids going down her back
And she also has long fingernails as a matter of fact
She has a Hello Kitty face on her neck
And a hello kitty gem on one of her blue fingernails
She has a matching loyalty tattoo just like her sister
She can look at her tattoo when she starts to miss her
Two pretty braids, keep on looking cute like you do
And always remember that Jesus loves you

LOVE SONG TO YOUR DADDY

My friend's son was so happy with his daddy one day
He ran and got out his guitar and began to play and sing
He said, Daddy I'm so happy with you
You cleaned, cleaned, cleaned
I'm so happy with you
I love you, Daddy, I love you
Love song to your daddy
Keep on singing happy songs like you do
And always remember that Jesus loves you

BROWN SUIT MAN

Brown suit man you are looking pretty cool
And you are also pretty handsome too
Dressed in your brown suit and your black brim
Wow you are really looking dressed to win
You are looking pretty fly
Looking like you can catch everyone's eye
Brown suit man, keep on looking cool
And always remember that Jesus loves you

ANOINTED DANCER

You are anointed by God this is true
From your continence to the way that you move
You touched the heart of God
And everyone else in the room
Our pastors were also pleased
And they are so very proud of you
God has great plans to use you
So stay focused in everything that you do
You're a blessing to this church
And always remember that Jesus loves you

SHINING LIGHT

When I look at you I see a light
Of course it is from our Lord and savior Jesus Christ
You have a glow that reflects His love
It touches everyone that you see
And oh you're such a blessing to me
You're a blessing to our church
And I'm sure to everyone who knows you
Shining light, thank you for all that you do
And always remember that Jesus loves you

PRAYING GRANDMA

She's a praying grandma and she is pretty cute too
She loves her grandson very much and he loves her too
I love to talk to her when I see her on Sunday
She loves the Lord and she always has nice things to say
Last week she came to church
With a beige colored sweater and a beige colored dress
Wow she really looked blessed
Praying grandma, keep on praying like you do
And always remember that Jesus loves you

SINGER AND DANCER

She's cute and she's sweet and she also loves to dance and sing
She is one of the sweetest girls in my class
She can really dance, and that's a fact
Singer and dancer, keep on doing the good job that you do
And always remember that Jesus loves you

NATURAL SMILE

There is a man that I have known for a while
He never frowns, I always see him smile
When I looked at his face today
I told him natural smile is a name that I picked for you
You inspire me, you really do
Natural smile, keep on sharing that smile like you do
And always remember that Jesus loves you

PEARL NECKLACE

My friend came to church today
She looked really pretty I must say
She had on a beautiful pearl necklace
And a pretty colored top
And she also wore a pretty clip in her hair
That really topped it all off
Pearl necklace, keep on looking cute like you do
And always remember that Jesus loves you

FLOWERS AND BUTTERFLIES

I saw a beautiful lady a while ago
She had pretty flowers in her hair
And pink earrings in her ears
And a bling heart around her neck
She looked so pretty I had to stare at her for a while
She was definitely one who could bring in a crowd
Flowers and butterflies, keep on looking beautiful like you do
And always remember that Jesus loves you

BASS SINGER

I know a bass singer and he is really cool
As a matter of fact, he is also handsome too
Everyone loves his deep voice
He testifies of God's love
And how he was healed because of Jesus' blood
Yes, bass singer is a blessed man
On Christ, the solid rock he stands
He also loves to pray
He has received miracle after miracle because of his faith
Bass singer, keep on doing the awesome job that you do
And always remember that Jesus loves you

THANK YOU FOR HELPING ME

May God bless you abundantly
I'm not a bit surprised why you are blessed like you are
You even give people who are down-and-out a ride in your car
You're quick to love and give people a hug
Whenever I'm around you I feel the Father's love
I love you and appreciate you too
And always remember that Jesus loves you

HELPFUL MAILMAN

You took time out of your busy schedule to help someone in need
That was such a kind thing for you to do, yes indeed
This world is a better place because of you
You not only deliver mail but you care about people too
Helpful mailman, I appreciate you
Keep on sharing kindness like you do
And always remember that Jesus loves you

THE GIRL WHO GAVE BACK 40 DOLLARS

I was at the laundry mat today when a man dropped some tokens
A girl picked them up and ran to give them back to him
And he said, thank you
I told her that was a nice thing for you to do
And she said I once saw someone lose forty dollars
And I gave it back to them too
Her mom said, I taught her well, she knows what to do
I thought, wow that's so amazing
Not many would do what you do
The girl who gave back forty dollars
Keep on being honest like you do
And always remember that Jesus loves you

TWO GORGEOUS LADIES

You're two gorgeous ladies this I can see
And also you're a blessing to everybody
From the smiles on your faces to your great personalities
Yes you both are amazing, amazing to me
I love your smiles and the way that you care for each other
I think it's really amazing how you honor and respect your mother

May God bless you both with everlasting life
Because you keep Jesus in the center of your life
You're both an example of a Godly mother and daughter
Of course it's because of God, your Heavenly Father
I pray that this poem touches both of you
And always remember that Jesus loves you

FOXY LADY

I saw you on Facebook today
You're very beautiful I must say
Beautiful hair in spiral curls
Beautiful blue blouse and a sharp necklace too
Let's not forget the beautiful brown eyes God has given to you
Yes, you're a foxy lady, this everyone can see
You're truly blessed, yes indeed
Your mom sure did a good job raising you
You take good care of yourself and respect your mother too
Foxy lady, keep on looking beautiful like you do
And always remember that Jesus loves you

BASS GUITAR PLAYER

There's a man I have known for almost 30 years
He plays the harmonica and the bass guitar too
His favorite music to play is gospel
And he also loves to play rhythm and blues
He's my brother in Christ, he is such a blessing to me
And also to all of our church family
One day he will teach me how to play the guitar
That's what I believe
We also sing together on the praise and worship team
It is very fun, and yes he can sing
Bass guitar player, keep on using your gifts like you do
And always remember that Jesus loves you

CREAM AND WHITE

I saw a man on Facebook today
He was very handsome I must say
He had on a white brim hat and a cream colored suit
And to top it off, he had on some white dress shoes
You have always been so kind
When I was younger your mom was a best friend of mine
Cream and white, keep on looking cool like you do
And always remember that Jesus loves you

HOLDING MY FIFTH GRANDCHILD

I was holding my fifth grandchild at church one day
We had a special time together, hey, hey, hey
He had a cute little smile on his face
He was happy to see grandma
He was happy to be in this place
He goes to just about everyone he sees
People like holding him because he's a happy baby
Fifth grandchild, you are special this is true
And always remember that Jesus loves you

SPRINT LADY

I appreciate you and how you tried to help me
You are one kind and compassionate young lady
Sprint should be very proud to have an employee like you
You care about your customers, you really do
And oh you have the most beautiful colored hair
And your necklace is really beautiful I declare
Sprint lady, I really enjoy talking to you
Keep on showing kindness and compassion like you do
And always remember that Jesus loves you

LOST 100 POUNDS

You're handsome
And also you're very cool
You're an awesome employee
And you're very kindhearted too
You lost 100 pounds
And I am so very proud of you
Now move forward and show others
What you have learned to do
Never give up on your dreams
That you have inside of you
And always remember that Jesus loves you

AUNTIE HOLDING NIECE

Look at auntie holding her niece
They both look so happy, happy yes indeed
They both have beautiful smiles, this I can see
Auntie and baby I love both of you
And always remember that Jesus loves you too

YOUR MOM TAUGHT YOU WELL

*You followed the path of righteousness
That your mom set before you
When you were faced with a big decision
Instead of listening to your flesh or the devil
You let your spirit lead you
I'm sure on that day God in heaven was happy
And your mom was happy too
You were blessed because you listened
To the voice of God inside of you*

*Only what we do for Christ will last
Your story made a lasting impression on me
And I'm sure many others too
When we hear a good story like this
We should share it and declare it*

*I'm sure giving back 25,000 was not an easy thing to do
But the values that your mom taught you
Were instilled deep inside of you
You have always been an inspiration to me
From your ability to hear from God
To the beautiful songs that you sing
You're beautiful inside and out this is true
And always remember that Jesus loves you*

THREE HANDSOME YOUNG MEN

*Three handsome young men in a picture on Facebook
They made a decision in their lives to do good
They honor their mom and they respect their dad
Godly examples are what they had
Handsome young men, keep on doing good like you do
And always remember that Jesus loves you*

GREAT BARBER

I went with my husband to get his hair cut on a beautiful Saturday
There was a guy there that he really likes to cut his hair
He really does a good job I declare
My husband is always happy after he does his hair
He doesn't want to go anywhere else, only right there
Great barber, keep on doing the great job that you do
You always make my husband's hair look so nice and smooth
I like your quiet personality and your good attitude
You're amazing this is true
And always remember that Jesus loves you

JOY BUBBLES

You are an amazing young lady
And you're very beautiful too
I am always so happy to be around you
God has given you so many joy bubbles
Everyone can feel them when they come around you
You're a blessing everywhere you go
Everyone can feel Jesus through you
You're really making a difference in everything you do
And always remember that Jesus loves you

ELEGANT FRAMES

My friend is really elegant in every way
From the clothes that she wears to the lifestyle she displays
She has blessed me many times in my life
Before I met her I walked around with low self-esteem
I wore whatever I had but it didn't look very neat
Now because of her, many times I look like a beauty queen
Then the other day she gave me some frames
I spread them out like a beautiful display
Elegant frames, thank you for always being a blessing to me
I love you and Jesus loves you too

FUN HAIR

I went to Mc Donald's a few days ago
While I was standing in line I saw a beautiful lady next to me
The thing I remember most was her beautiful long blonde hair
It was so pretty and clean
In my imagination I began to dream
If I had all that long hair
I would have many different styles I declare
Her hair looked so fun to me
I could see myself braiding it or putting it up in a bun
Or just twirling it having all kinds of fun
Fun hair, enjoy the long hair that God has given to you
And always remember that Jesus loves you

BLUE FLOWER DRESS

I was at the laundromat on Saturday
Washing clothes after a busy day
I turned around and coming in the door behind me
Was a beautiful mother and her cute one year old baby girl
She had on a very pretty flowered dress
And pretty pink shoes that had flowers on them too
She looked like she'd just came out of a magazine
She had a smile so bright for all the world to see
Seeing her face made be very happy
Thank you God for loving me through that precious one year old baby
Blue flower dress, keep on looking beautiful like you do
And always remember that Jesus loves you

HE DANCES WITH HIS DADDY

He dances with his daddy, oh what a special thing to see
Oh how precious, precious, precious, yes indeed
The memories that you make with him
He will think on them as he grows up again and again
It's awesome that you take time with your son
I can see that he's your special son
The bond between you two is because Jesus in you
He dances with his daddy
Keep on dancing with your daddy like you do
And always remember that Jesus loves you

ACTOR AND COMEDIAN

He's young and handsome just like his dad
He's one of the awesome kids in my class
And he loves acting too
Maybe when he grows up
He could make a lot of money doing what he loves to do
Actor and comedian, keep on loving Jesus
And doing what you love to do
And always remember that Jesus loves you

MASTER CHEF

Your hamburgers and hot dogs were a big hit
You're the greatest master chef, I'm sure of it
You cooked for all of us in the hot sun
We grubbed on the food and had a lot of fun
At the next outing we will be looking for you
Because you're the greatest at what you do
Master chef, keep on doing the good job that you do
And always remember that Jesus loves you

AMAZING BLING BLING BLOUSE

There's a lady I have known for quite a while
She has a great personality and a beautiful smile
She came to church one day
She had a beautiful bling bling blouse on, hey, hey, hey
It sparkled and shined
She really looked fine
Amazing bling bling blouse
Keep on looking cute like you do
And always remember that Jesus loves you

COOL BLONDE HAIRCUT

There's a handsome boy in my class
He is also really cool as a matter of fact
I love his happy smile and his cool blonde haircut too
He loves coming to church with his mom
And she loves being there with him too
Cool blonde haircut
Keep on looking cool like you do
And always remember that Jesus loves you

STONE NECKLACE AND MATCHING EARRINGS

I have known a lady for many years
She is very kind and very dear
She has a beautiful smile and a great personality too
She's the kind of person anyone would love to call their friend
She will be with you through thick and thin
Today she had on a stone necklace and matching earrings too
I told her, wow your jewelry really looks good on you

RHYTHM GUITAR PLAYER/POLICE SERGEANT

There's a man I have known for almost 30 years
He plays the rhythm guitar and he sings good too
He loves to share the love of Jesus with anyone he gets a chance to
Police Sergeant, I appreciate everything that you do
In our church and on the police force too
This world is a better place
Because of a loyal Police Sergeant like you
And I'm sure everyone at our church feels the same way too
Keep up the good job that you do
And always remember that Jesus loves you

RHINESTONE SHIRT

My friend sat next to me in church today
She had on a very beautiful array
She had on a rhinestone black shirt
With rhinestone earrings too
And on top of all of that
She also had rhinestones on top of her shoes
Rhinestone shirt, keep on looking cute like you do
You got it going on, you know that you do
You're a fashionable young lady
And you're very precious too
And always remember that Jesus loves you

FOLDING CLOTHES

I was washing clothes on Sunday
When I saw a beautiful lady and her daughter in front of me
She was showing her daughter how to fold clothes
She had a lot of patience it really showed
They had fun as they folded clothes together
It was a beautiful day, it was sun-shiny weather
Oh how it brought back precious memories
When I was a little girl with my mommy and me
Hang on to these precious times
Because when they grow up you'll only see your children sometimes
Folding clothes, keep on making memories like you do
And always remember that Jesus loves you

HANDSOME BROTHER

My brother is handsome and he is also cool
On top of all that he's a hard worker too
You have taken care of the house and beautified the yard too
Just imagine Momma looking down from heaven
And saying, son I'm so proud of you
I love your hats, suits, and your bling bling
You go my brother, do your thing
Handsome brother, keep on doing the good job that you do
And always remember that Jesus loves you

HAPPY STICKS AND CUTIE

Happy Sticks is a kind man
And his wife is a cutie too
I have known them for many years
And they have always been kind to me too
Happy Sticks loves to play the drums
And he is very good at it too
His wife is a wonderful young lady
And she has a very pleasant attitude
Whenever I see her smile, she makes me smile too
Happy Sticks and Cutie
You're both a blessing to everyone who comes around you
And always remember that Jesus loves you

DEGREES

Congrats beautiful lady
What a great accomplishment for you
You received your degree and your mom is so very proud of you
Finally, all of your hard work has paid off
You should be proud of yourself too
Keep on moving forward, great things await you
And always remember that Jesus loves you

DRESSED IN PINSTRIPE AND WHITE

I saw a little boy on my Facebook page one day
He was looking pretty fly I must say
He had on a pinstripe suit and a pinstripe hat
And also a pinstripe tie as a matter of fact
Then he had on a white shirt and white tennis shoes
He looked like a little model in my eyes
If he was in a contest he would definitely win first prize
Dressed in pinstripe and white
Keep on looking cool like you do
And always remember that Jesus loves you

SHE CARRIES HER AGE WELL

I met a lady today
She was very beautiful I must say
She had a beautiful new baby boy
He had a head full of curls
Her special baby boy was a big part of her world
I couldn't believe that she was in her thirties
She carries her age well, keep on looking beautiful like you do
And always remember that Jesus loves you

BOOM BOX SHIRT

There's a boy who comes to church
Sometimes he's in my class and sometimes he's not
He loves to have fun and he loves to laugh a lot
He also loves to learn about Jesus too
Most of the time he has a big smile on his face
When I see him smile he makes me smile too
Smiling seems to be something kids like to do
Boom box shirt, keep on having fun like you do
And always remember that Jesus loves you

CROSS MATCHES CLOTHES

I met a lady in the waiting room one day
She was very beautiful I must say
She had a beautiful colorful cross on her arm
And also a matching dress on
But what made me notice her right away
Was her conversation about God's word, hey, hey, hey
Cross matches clothes
Keep on sharing the love of God like you do
And always remember that Jesus loves you

NESTLE COFFEE MAN

He always comes to help us when we call
No matter how big the job is or how small
He always greets us with a smile on his face
He gives me tips to take care of the coffee machine
Including how to keep it nice and clean
Nestle coffee man, keep on doing the good job that you do
And always remember that Jesus loves you

A CIRCLE OF CATS

There is a girl that I met a while ago
She is very beautiful don't you know
The other day she had on a T-shirt with a circle of cats
I got really excited and took a picture of that
The cats were many different colors, it was cool
I would like to have a T-shirt like that too
Seeing that shirt brought back memories when I was a little girl
At that time cats were a big part of my world
Circle of cats, I appreciate you
And always remember that Jesus loves you

GRANDPA AND GRANDSON

Grandpa holding his fifth grandchild after church one Sunday
They both have big happy smiles upon their face
Grandpa loves grandson and grandson loves him too
Also they both are very handsome too
Grandpa and grandson, keep on loving each other like you do
And always remember that Jesus loves you

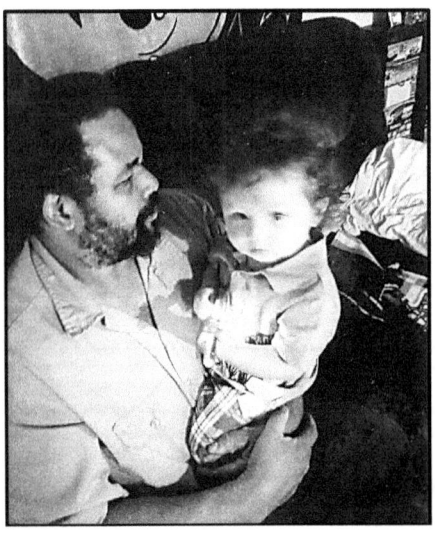

INTELLIGENT GIRL

You're one intelligent girl this is true
And you're also very beautiful too
God has given a good mind to you
You did a great job all throughout school
And your mom is so very proud of you
Intelligent girl, you can do whatever you set your mind to do
If you dare to keep dreaming, you will keep achieving
There is nothing that is impossible for you
And always remember that Jesus loves you

MEDIA MAN

There's a man I have known for a little while
He is very smart with the media and many other things too
He shares the word from our church on Facebook and YouTube
And he also created the church website too
He also runs the camera or whatever he is needed to do
Media man, thanks for all that you do
And always remember that Jesus loves you

GREAT SENSE OF HUMOR

I went to the Family Dollar store the other day
There was a kind man that waited on me
He had a great sense of humor I must say
He not only waited on me
But he made me laugh constantly
He had a long ponytail in his hair
He also had a cheerful smile I declare
Great sense of humor, keep on making customers happy like you do
And always remember that Jesus loves you

HANDSOME GUY WITH A BLACK BOWTIE

I was at church one Sunday, when I turned around who did I see?
A handsome guy with a bowtie standing in front of me
I thought, wow he is handsome and he looks nice too
He is glad to be in the house of God
And we are glad to have you here too
Come to find out his grandma comes here too
Then my friend turned around and a big smile came on her face
She watched him when he was a little baby
She was very happy, you could tell by the look on her face
Now he comes every week
We are blessed to see him, yes indeed
Handsome guy with a bowtie
Keep on looking fine like you do
And always remember that Jesus loves you

STYLING GRANDMA

I saw a beautiful lady tonight
She had on cute blue jeans
And she had some of the most beautiful blue eyes
I told her, I got a name for you
Styling grandma is what I'll call you
She smiled and leaned to the side
Then we gave each other a hug and a big smile
Styling grandma, keep on looking cute like you do
And always remember that Jesus loves you

ANGELIC VOICES

My ears and my heart were so touched
The minute they opened their mouths I felt God's love
Wow angelic voices were in our church
At that moment I felt like heaven had come down to earth
They are so anointed, yes they are
They love God with all of their hearts
I recorded them as they began to sing
So I could hear their voices over and over again

Wow angelic voices in our church
At that moment I felt like heaven had come down to earth
They are my sisters in the Lord and my special friends
I am so glad I'm starting to have a special relationship with them
Angelic voices, keep on sharing your beautiful voices like you do
And always remember that Jesus loves you

FISHER OF SOULS

You heard the message loud and clear
Winning souls for Christ rings through your ears
People see the difference that Jesus makes in your life
Even though you have been through very difficult times
You love Jesus with all of your heart
I could tell that about you right from the start
Fisher of souls, keep on doing what God has called you to do
And always remember that Jesus loves you

BEAUTIFUL DESIGNS

There's a beautiful lady I met a while ago
She is very gifted don't you know
She made beautiful designs on two floors in her house
I was so excited when I saw them I said, wow, with a shout
On top of all of that she makes beautiful T-shirts too
And they have lots of bling bling, yes they are really cool
Oh how I would like to create with her someday
Then we could have fun together, hey, hey, hey
Beautiful designs, keep on making beautiful things like you do
And always remember that Jesus loves you

A's WITH HONORS

You're a beautiful young lady
And you're very friendly too
I appreciate how you always listen in class
You never give me any attitude
A's with honors, your mom is very proud of you
You go beautiful young lady
Keep on doing what you do
And always remember that Jesus Christ loves you

PRETTY GIRL WITH PINK HAIR

I saw a pretty girl with pink hair
And she had a big beautiful black and white flower in her hair
She looked really cute I declare
She also had some cool tattoos, they were pretty colorful too
Pretty girl with pink hair, keep on looking cute like you do
And always remember that Jesus loves you

BEAUTIFUL BODY BUILDER

She's beautiful, she's sweet
And she is also very unique
God created her in a special way
She is one of my sisters in the Lord I'm glad to say
She has beautiful hair and she's a great body builder too
She also has her own beauty salon for me and for you
Beautiful body builder keep on doing what you do
And always remember that Jesus loves you

PURPLE AND BLACK

There was a boy in my class last week
He was very handsome and very sweet
I have known him ever since he was a baby boy
He has a special place in my heart that's for sure
He was dressed in black and purple that day
He really looked good, hey, hey, hey
Black and purple, keep on looking handsome like you do
And always remember that Jesus loves you

HAPPY SECOND ANNIVERSARY

Happy second anniversary to a beautiful husband and wife
Outside enjoying the beautiful creation that God made for you
You're all looking nice
I love your beautiful smiles and your wonderful attitudes
I pray many happier anniversaries for both of you
I love you both very much and Jesus also loves you too
Once again happy anniversary and congrats to you

JOY TO MY HEART

I met a girl when she was real young
She loves to learn about Jesus and she loves to have fun
The Bible says that we can learn a lot from kids
She has a lot of wisdom in her heart for sure
One day I was trying to find a song on YouTube for us to sing
And she told me, you like to sing, well sing, your own song then
I thought, wow that's good advice coming from you
Next time that's just what I will do
Joy to my heart, keep on being a blessing to me—I love you
And always remember that Jesus loves you too

BLUE AND BLACK FAITH SHIRT

There's a lady I have known for a while
She has a great personality and a beautiful smile
She loves to braid hair
And she is very good at it I declare
She has three beautiful girls and a wonderful boy
I am so happy for her, hey, hey, hey
I love your blue and black faith shirt, it's really cool
And I like the way you represent Jesus like you do
You love Jesus and I love Him too
That is something we have in common between us two
Blue and black faith shirt
Keep on making beautiful braids like you do
And always remember that Jesus loves you

ANOINTED DRUMMER

I have known you since you were a baby
And you were always amazing to me
Back then you were just cute
But now you are as fine as can be
And oh how you are anointed to play those drums
As you sit there in your seat
You are definitely called by God, this everyone can see
Out of all the drummers in the world you are my favorite one
Anointed drummer, keep on letting the spirit of God use you
And always remember that Jesus loves you

INDIAN DRESS AND BLING BLING JEWELRY

There's a lady I have known for a while
She always says hi and always has a smile
She also loves to give me a hug
Because she cares for me as her friend
And she likes to share God's love
One day she had on a beautiful Indian dress
And bling bling jewelry too
I told her, I love your Indian dress
And your bling bling jewelry too
Indian dress and bling bling jewelry, thanks for being my friend
I appreciate you
And always remember that Jesus loves you

TWIN SISTERS

You're two beautiful young ladies
And you're very special too
You both have kind hearts and great attitudes
You were both kind to me in school
And you're still kind to me today too
Maybe because we have a connection with Jesus
You know He's the truth, the light, and the way
Twin sisters, everyone around you loves you
And always remember that Jesus loves you too

CARING HEART

You care for people who are down and out
You provide them with clothing
You don't want to see them go without
God has given you a kind and compassionate heart
You want to see people make it
You don't want them to fall apart
Thank you for all the people that you help, including me
I appreciate you
And always remember that Jesus loves you

PERFECT FRENCH BRAIDS

Perfect French braids all lined in a row
Her mommy did a great job doing her hair don't you know
Cute little beads on the end of all of her braids
And a pretty pink and yellow top, wow she really looks amazing
Perfect French braids, keep on looking beautiful like you do
And always remember that Jesus loves you

GODLY EXAMPLES

They are my pastors this is true
I love them very much, yes I do
They have been with me through thick and thin
And they have loved me unconditionally again and again
I've never seen or felt the real love of God before I met them
They're Godly examples I will proclaim
And they love to praise Jesus and bless His name

God, thank you for pastors who pray for me, teach me, correct me
Challenge me, encourage me, minister to me, sacrifice for me
Stand in the gap for me, encourage me to be all that I can be
Fast with me and for me and our church family
God help me rise up and go forward in you
Like my Godly examples have shown me and taught me to do
Godly examples, I love you
And always remember that Jesus loves you too

MOTHER AND DAUGHTER BLING BLING

You both are amazing, amazing to me
And I love your wonderful bling bling
The tops that you make to magnify our Lord
Are some of the most amazing and beautiful tops in the whole world
Mother and daughter bling bling, keep on doing what you do
And always remember that Jesus loves you

WHITE LACE PANTS

I saw a lady at church today
She is very beautiful I must say
She had some beautiful white lace pants on
And a pretty purple blouse too
I told her, I really like your pants
And your purple blouse too
She smiled and went on her way
I think I made her happy that day
White lace pants, keep on looking beautiful like you do
And always remember that Jesus loves you

BLING BLING FLOWER MAN

He passed out beautiful bling bling flowers one day
Of course first he gave some to his beautiful fiancé
My heart was touched at the kind thing he did
I just had to thank him over and over again
Bling bling flower man, keep on doing the kind things that you do
And always remember that Jesus loves you

TRIBUTE TO OUR CHURCH GRANDMA

She loved everyone like they were her own kids
She loved to give us all hugs and a big oh smiley grin
She told everyone that they were her favorite one
And she was really proud of her preacher man son
Years have come and gone and I still miss you
You loved to hear me sing and you always told me good job
You made the best sugar cookies that I have ever had in my life
I couldn't just eat one, I had to come back twice
I remember when we used to have cell groups in your home
I felt accepted by you, I felt right at home
You showed your son a real relationship with God for doing this
We are all blessed week after week and all year long
I love you church grandma and many other do too
I'm sure you're enjoying Jesus and He's enjoying you too

UNIQUE ARTIST

The creativity of God runs all through you
You're amazing this is true
God blessed you with a gift to create
I can see it every time I look at your face
Yes, you're unique, you're so special to God
And I think that it is really amazing
How you love and honor your dad and your mom
Your pictures are amazing and they look so real
You're not a fake, you're the real deal
Your pictures have such deep thought
You can tell your gift is from your Father God
Unique artist, keep on letting God use you
And always remember that Jesus loves you

CUTE SHOES AND FLOWERED DRESS

My friend looked so cute on Sunday
She had on some cute shoes and a beautiful flowered dress
I really liked her outfit, I was really impressed
She always looks nice in everything that she wears
And she has a heart full of love that shows how much she cares
Cute shoes and flowered dress
Keep on looking beautiful like you do
And always remember that Jesus loves you

515

515 is very special to me
He is my creative son yes indeed
He brought out his own clothing line
I must say he looks mighty fine
I love him and he loves me
515, keep on doing what you do
And always remember that Jesus loves you

MY GENTLE GIANT

He is 6 foot 7 and he's as kind as can be
Yes, God gave a gentle giant to me
As he holds his baby in his arms
You can feel the love that radiates from his heart
Gentle giant, keep up the good job being a father like you do
And always remember that Jesus loves you

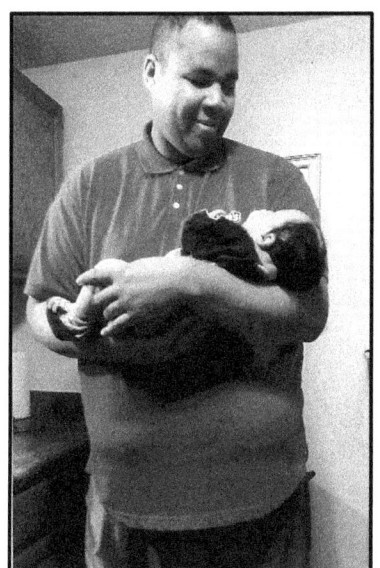

SWEATPANTS WITH THE WORD LOVE IN BLING

I was at the library the other day
When a beautiful lady came and sat beside me
She had on a pretty pink tank top and cute pink flip flops too
And she had on some cute green sweatpants
With the word "love" in bling, oh she looked really cute
Sweatpants with the word "love" in bling
Keep on looking cute like you do
And always remember that Jesus loves you

SERVICE TECH

I met a man a week ago
He was very kind don't you know
He was at my work place making sure the kitchen things
And the ice machine were in good condition
He took his time and he did it right like any service tech should do
He also had a smile on his face and a good attitude
Service tech, thanks for all that you do
And always remember that Jesus loves you

MOMMA'S HELPER

You're a beautiful young lady, and you're very special too
You helped clean the apartment when your mom was sick
And you help her many other times too
You also help watch your brother and your younger cousin too
You love Jesus and you love praising Him too
Thanks again for the beautiful poem that I received from you
Momma's helper, keep on doing the good job that you do
And always remember that Jesus loves you

PHARMACY TEAM

Pharmacy team you're so amazing to me
And I appreciate your great hospitality
Through the years when I came to get help to relieve pain
You all stepped up to help me again and again
One of the greatest core values that I see in you is compassion
When people who are hurting come to you, you don't turn them away
You never get a second chance to make a first impression
I will always remember the kindness I received form you
And always remember that Jesus loves you

PURPLE SHIRT AND PRETTY PURPLE EARRINGS

You look so beautiful today
In your purple shirt and your pretty purple earrings
And your sunglasses are also very cool I must say
Your daughter is very beautiful
And your granddaughter is very beautiful too
I can tell that they both get their good looks from you
Purple shirt and pretty purple earrings
Keep on looking cute like you do
And always remember that Jesus loves you

TEACHER/PROOFREADER

There's a lady I have known for many years
She is my proofreader for many of my books
And also my teacher too
She has taught me and is teaching me things
That I don't remember or never knew
She is a blessing to me and to many others too
By the way, she also writes poetry
There is a connection between us two
Teacher/Proofreader, thanks for all that you do
And always remember that Jesus loves you

MINISTRY WOMAN

Thank you for taking time to teach me
Even when your life for God is really busy
You have a heart after God
I could see it through the years being in your ministry
Even though sometime I didn't want to hear what you said
Years later the wisdom from God that you share
Is still in my heart and in my head
I will remember you in every book that I write
Because it is coming true
What God told you to speak over me that night
I love you, ministry woman, I do
And always remember that Jesus loves you too

GRANDMA AND GRANDSON

Grandma and grandson working in the kitchen
Getting the batter ready for some yummy fried chicken
Dipping it in some eggs and some seasoned flour too
Making memories together is a great thing to do

MY GRANDDAUGHTER

*You're precious, precious, precious, my dear
And I love the beautiful flowers in your hair
You get your good looks from your mom and dad
You are one beautiful girl that they had
Granddaughter, keep on looking beautiful like you do
And always remember that Jesus loves you*

TO MY PUBLISHER BETH

*You are an amazing publisher this I can see
You came and helped me even when I was with another company
I am so excited to work with you
I'm looking for great success between me and you
I prayed for honest help and God sent me you
I pray that 100-fold blessing will come back to you
Thank you for caring and God bless you*

ABOUT THE AUTHOR

Maryann Tolson has been writing songs since 2000. In the past seven months, God has blessed her with a creative gift of poetry. She is inspired first of all by God, and then by the beauty of creation. She loves encouraging people with kind words. Some poems are short and some are long, but they all have meaning. As she encourages others, she herself is encouraged.

Maryann is also the author of *My Spiritual Journey in Music*. She is currently working on several other books.

Maryann loves to hear from readers. You can reach her at: maryanntolson12@gmail.com

www.ingramcontent.com/pod-product-compliance
Lightning Source LLC
LaVergne TN
LVHW021400080426
835508LV00020B/2378